Al —

Keep using the MMM!

D1277553

Transforming Your Aging Brain

with the Multi-Modal Method

A joyful way to enhance cognition, memory and well being

Linda S. Stoler, M.A., CCC-SLP

and Gretchen L. Espinetti, Ph.D.

Transforming Your Aging Brain
ISBN: 978-0-9854381-9-7

Project coordination and editing by Will Stoler.

Content editing, interior design and pagination by On-Target Words (www.ontargetwords.com)

Cover design, layout, photographs and interior photographs by Peter B. Wilder

Please contact us: Brainysounds, LLC
Mailing address: 7 Sabor de Sal Road
                        St. Augustine, FL   32080
Phone: 802-777-4299
Email address: willstoler@gmail.com
Website   http://transformingyouragingbrain.com

WC Publishing
an On-Target Words company

What people are saying . . .

Thanks for the Great Information...
Very different than I expected it to be. It gave a crash course on the parts and functions of the brain and gave ways to improve the efficiency of each part. Not surprisingly, almost everything to improve brain function was common sense stuff that we already know, yet rarely do. My daily life will now include many of these simple tasks because any chance of reducing dementia and Alzheimer's disease is well worth my time.
— Allison Davis, Reviewer

Good Information...
I found this book to be very informative. I do not normally gravitate to self-help books, but found this to be a combination of text book/self-help that was surprisingly easy to read. There were some suggestions for simple practices and exercises that would be easy to follow in everyday life.
— Debbie Kilduff, Teacher

This Book Gives Wonderful Perspective...
Although I am still relatively young, having many years of experience working in long term care facilities, this book gives wonderful perspective on many levels... I would recommend this book to any brain conscious person of any age to supplement a long and happy existence.
— Wolfess Rose, Healthcare Provider

Refreshing & Meaningful...
When I was younger, I had an elderly grandmother who had Alzheimer's disease. I really feel that if maybe a few months before she was diagnosed, if she had read this, she still might have had a chance. The book suggests that people ages 50 and over should read, and I am a younger person. Even my young brain felt refreshed and energized after this read. It's interesting and informational. Give this one a good look!
— Dannie Moffit, Grandson

Dedicated to Linda's mother, "Flo" and Gretchen's dad, "Hank."

They remain the inspiration for this book.

Focus and Discussion Questions for Readers of
Transforming Your Aging Brain

The following four questions are intended to spark a discussion and serve as a guide for those people who wish to have a deeper understanding of how to integrate the principles [Music, manual motion (sign language), mindful meditation (to include Saa Taa Naa Maa) and awareness, alignment, yoga and breathing, cross lateralization, yawning, smiling, tapping, metacognition, focus and attention, visualization, movement/dance, universal energy, obstacle thinking, XXX Change, authenticity, sensory awareness, nutrition, physical exercise, healthy lifestyle choices, gratitude, joy, wisdom, creativity, memory and leaving a legacy] outlined in *TYAB* in their daily lives.

Using *TYAB* as a guide, review one session or related practice at a time, **applying each question to the individual segment**:

1. What new insights did you uncover?
2. How are you integrating this modality or practice into your daily life?
3. What changes in attitude, perspective or physical well-being are you now experiencing as a result of this work?
4. What additional guidance do you need to help engage in these modalities/practices daily?

Table of Contents

Foreword: Our Genesis

Your inner purpose is to awaken. You share that purpose with every other person on the planet-because it is the purpose of humanity.
Eckhart Tolle

This book, and indeed, our seminars, will contain terms and information that may be unfamiliar to many of you. We promise to explain so that you'll understand what's going on in your brain, how best to support good brain-function, and what things you might enjoy trying to stimulate your brain to grow healthier day by day.

This information is far from new and we are delighted to tell you that ancient traditional modalities including music, movement, manual motion (sign language) and mindful meditation are effective tools for holistic wellness. When utilized together, they support and enhance positive brain transformation.

The Multi-Modal Method (MMM), was not accidentally discovered. Linda has worked with people in the domain of speech-language pathology and education for more than forty-five years. She studied research by neuroscience experts regarding brain function and health, and observed, as a woman of science and passion can, that elders benefit in many of the same ways that children do when exposed to her multi-modal method.

Watching the joy on her aging mother's face when she heard the music and moved to the rhythms, Linda realized that it was possible to positively impact the largest aging population on record.

As a team, we've all observed the decline of our loved ones in terms of memory, health, socializing and spirituality. All of us can think of how parents, grandparents, aunts, uncles, siblings and friends age and experience these areas of diminished capacity. As caregivers committed to changing the quality of life for ourselves and our loved ones, these observations have been both challenging and inspiring as we navigate the journey of how to be the best "care partners" for all.

Every day, 10,000 Baby Boomers retire. Every 68 seconds someone is diagnosed with some form of dementia, including Alzheimer's. Sharing the heartfelt moments of our loved ones' lives has helped us see the urgent need for an immediate paradigm shift from the traditional ways of viewing and assisting our aging population. The world is moving at an accelerated pace. A profound and global awareness of the urgency to change our values and attitudes towards elders and aging is what is needed to positively impact aging around the world. Contrary to older schools of thought, newer research has proven that the aging brain is able to remain viable, flexible and joyful as it encounters new activities to expand memory, focus and attention! It is true that "old dogs" can learn new things.

Our state of consciousness is being transformed as we awaken to the changes within ourselves. Along this journey, we have been fortunate to find those who share a common vision for their parents' lives, their own lives and for generations to come. Such is the case for all of us: Linda, Gretchen, Will, Celeste, Peter and our many supporters. We're committed to developing a new way to transform the aging process by inspiring elders with a sense of value, voice and vision for the future.

You're going to hear and see the word *neuroplasticity* in this book a lot. We can't talk about changes in our brains without it! *Plasticity* essentially means *change*. In our brains, neurons, glia, and vascular cells are all involved in neuroplasticity.

Over a person's lifetime, these changes occur under a variety of conditions. For example: normal development of the immature brain into adulthood; when it's necessary to adapt to lost or damaged functionality, such as recovery from a stroke or injuries from an accident; and when new meaningful experiences promote changes in the brain.

Through neuroplasticity we *can* constantly and positively evolve. By uncovering our innate creativity, true passions, and joy we become actively involved in promoting positive, intentional brain stimulation and holistic wellbeing. We can help to slow the decline of our mental abilities (no matter what age) and minimize the debilitating aspects associated with dementia and Alzheimer's.

It is our intention in this book to share with you the Multi-Modal Method (MMM) which is supported by the latest neuroscience research. For more information, please see the Helpful Resources page at the back of the book.

Here is your personal invitation to transform your quality of life by rewiring your aging brain!

Transforming Your Aging Brain

*An invitation
To awaken
With celebration,
Your aging brain!
Attention and repetition
Lead to transformation:
The facts explain
Old patterns that do not matter
Will leave your brain—
Not to remain...
Replaced with new thoughts and joyful feelings
These are ways to change your brain!
Join the journey to explore
This new, exciting terrain.
Here's your chance:
Sing, sign, and dance—
Meditate, visualize
Rewire your brain
To change!*

The Brain and Our Senses

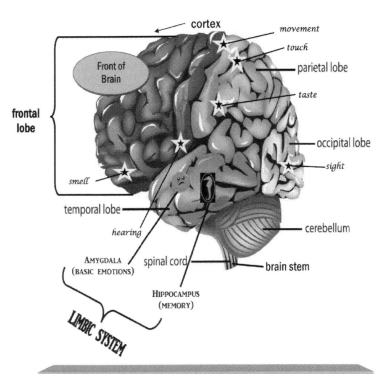

"The Brain and Our Senses"

- Amygdala and Hippocampus are located deep within the brain
- Senses (in italics) reside in these areas of the brain
- Frontal lobe is the entire Front of Brain area

I

Session One: The Brain and Neuroplasticity

Your brain never loses the power to transform itself based on experiences.
Richard Restak

The brain is the crown jewel of the human body.
NIH-National Institute of Health

There are more brain connections than stars in the sky. We have approximately 100 billion brain cells and 1,000 trillion neuron connections, many more than experts once thought. The ability of the brain to create new connections and reorganize itself is called *neuroplasticity.*

The process of brain reorganization takes place by "axonal sprouting" as explained by Jon Kabat-Zinn. Undamaged axons grow new nerve endings to reconnect neurons, which form new neural pathways. This is similar to when we replace or repair a damaged electrical cord.

Long-held scientific beliefs have asserted that the brain stopped developing after age twenty-one. Extensive research in the field of neuroscience, now supports our understanding that the brain continues to change and grow throughout our lives. We experience "pruning" (elimination of existing synapses), "neurogenesis" (growth of new brain cells) and "myelinization"(strengthening of existing neural pathways).

A stimulated brain grows new connections in every conceivable way. Innovative ideas and experiences allow the brain to create new wiring. The ability to direct and focus attention can shape the brain's firing patterns.

Through the power of neuroplasticity, attention to specific skills will change neural connections. Focus, novelty, reward, emotional arousal, and depth of meaning all promote "new" firing in the brain.

When we concentrate on positive outcomes in our lives, they can become the new landscape of our brain. Our attention, intention, and disciplined repetition create these connections. When the brain's cells are firing, the brain chemicals *dopamine* and *acetylcholine* help support focus and memory. When we exercise our brain in new ways, we create greater neuron interconnection and adaptation, allowing individuals the opportunity to keep changing and improving, no matter their age. We can also nurture an undeveloped set of *circuits*. This is how the brain can be *rewired*.

The human brain is genetically and socially predisposed for language, music and spirituality. During our lifetime, the brain continues to evolve, allowing us to experience more positive emotions as we mature. According to George Vaillant (who directed Harvard's famous Longitudinal Study of Adult Development for thirty-five years) frontal lobes become wired to the limbic system, which regulates emotion and memory. That means that planning is therefore linked to passion!

The Neocortex and its Four Lobes

Our *neocortex* distinguishes us from other known vertebrates on the planet. It is, in terms of evolution, the newest (*neo*) portion of the *cerebral cortex* and serves as the connection highway for higher mental functions.

According to Roger Penrose and Carl Sagan, "The human neocortex is more complex than a galaxy." Almost everything you see when you look at the brain from the top or sides is the neocortex.

Ninety percent of the cerebral cortex is the neocortex—a thin, gray membrane, which surrounds the deeper, white matter in the brain.

Let's create a picture of the major players in our brain. If we divide the brain in half like a grapefruit, those halves are called cerebral hemispheres (from the Latin words meaning *brain* and *halved sphere*, respectively).

Within each of the left and right hemispheres, the brain is divided into four major lobes or sections: the *frontal (top front), parietal (top middle), occipital* (back) and *temporal (lower)*. Refer to the diagram of the brain on page 6 to help clarify each of these.

Each of those sections within the brain is important for specific purposes. Therefore, we can access specific areas of the brain by adjusting the intensity of focus (volume) up or down in a specific area of the brain, in order to achieve a particular outcome. This is an *intentional adjustment.*

For example, if we want to improve our creative focus, we "turn up" the volume in the back of the brain. If we want greater focus and planning ability, we turn the volume up in the front of the brain. In order to calm our mind and body, we turn down the volume in the amygdala. By adjusting the volume in the limbic system, we can establish a stronger feeling of joy, peace and well being because that is where our emotions reside.

We're explaining specific areas of the brain so that we can understand how transforming our aging brain is certainly something we can do!

The frontal lobe includes all of the neocortex from the front, just behind the face. It is considered the hub or "CEO" of the brain, and is vitally responsible for our behavior, motor skills, and problem-solving ability. In the frontal cortex, a "hotbed" of neurons respond to both external and internal stimuli. The frontal lobe controls personality, movement, emotions and long-term memory.

In the 1800s, a railroad foreman named Phineas Gage sustained a horrible injury to his frontal lobe when a heavy iron pole was driven into his head. His family and friends noted that though he physically survived the accident, Phineas had been transformed from a quiet, gentle and hardworking man into one who was mean and unmotivated until the day he died. This case was one of the earliest documented cases studied by medical and psychiatric doctors that dealt with the functions of the frontal lobe.

The *frontal cortex* is extremely important in terms of our behavior. This part of the brain gives us the appropriate response to both external and internal stimuli. It's also critical to assist with learning, memory, attention and motivation because it plays a major role in working memory. In the frontal cortex we make our "executive decisions" regarding things like long and short-term planning.

From this portion of our brain, we concentrate on attention and focus. Dr. Daniel

Siegel at UCLA indicates that focus and attention harness the mind, direct energy and information, change synaptic connections, and stimulate neural growth.

In front of the frontal lobe is a section of the brain known in the scientific world, as the *prefrontal cortex*. Simply defined by Webster's dictionary, it's the gray matter in *front* of the frontal lobe that is highly developed in humans and plays a role in the regulation of complex cognitive, emotional and behavioral functioning.

It's here that we gain insight into our inner world. The prefrontal cortex helps us with contemplation, reflection, planning, dreams, imagination, redirection and reshaping of our brain.

The *parietal lobe* integrates sight, sound, and touch information, sensation, perception and spatial awareness. It resides in the back of the cortex.

The *occipital lobe* is located behind the cortex near the cerebellum and receives visual information from the retina. If you have just seen a lion heading your way, you will be getting ready to respond because the occipital lobe has just sent that image to your temporal and parietal lobe for processing. Working together, your cerebral cortex is getting together the information that you need to get out of the way of that lion.

The *temporal lobe* is responsible for auditory as well as visual processing. If the lion roared, that information will have been communicated to the cortex as well.

Remember that earlier we pointed out that emotions reside in the limbic system. Science now understands that the stronger the emotion evoked at the time of an event, the stronger the memory, even over long periods of time. Retention of memory is related to elevated emotion. If you've ever been frightened by a lion, you won't forget one tiny detail of that experience!

Linked to the frontal cortex is the *limbic system*.

Limbic System

The limbic system is a complex set of structures that lies on both sides of the *thalamus* (a walnut-shaped structure perched on top of the brainstem) which is just under the cerebrum. It's responsible for our emotions and the formation of memories. In addition, it is the primary neurological agent for human spirituality, which is rooted in relationship. It operates much like a switchboard of information to the cerebral cortex.

Mystical experience and positive emotions such as love, compassion, joy, empathy, and forgiveness are rooted in the limbic system. The limbic system and cortex communicate back and forth.

Through the use of our Multi-Modal Method tools—music, movement, manual motion (sign language) and mindful meditation, we can *exchange* our negative emotions for elevated feelings and thoughts.

In Session Six we'll explain our effective process of exchanging emotions. This process strengthens positive patterns, thoughts and neural connections. Dr. Daniel Amen, in *Change Your Brain*, suggests we can exchange our "ANTS" (auto negative thoughts) for positive thoughts such as love, peace, faith, and gratitude.

Many studies have shown that we can change our brain's chemistry by changing how our brain interprets the data it receives from the limbic system. Two essential parts of the limbic system worth mentioning for our purposes in transforming our aging brains, are the *hippocampus* and the *amygdala*.

Hippocampus

The hippocampus (hip´-po-kam-pus) is located in the temporal lobe and is the part of the limbic system which deals with emotions. It resides in both the left and right hemispheres of the brain and directs incoming memory from the senses to long-term memory in the cortex. It's important for learning as well as memory and emotions.

Short-term memory is related to the hippocampus and the temporal lobes. The hippocampus organizes, sorts, and processes information in your mind "at the moment" before routing that information to areas of the cortex to be stored for long-term memory.

It has been noted that if either the left or the right side of the hippocampus is damaged, memory function will continue almost as though no damage has occurred.

Amygdala

The amygdala (a-mig´-da-la), deep within the temporal lobe, lying in the center of the limbic system, is the least evolved part of our brain. It is a powerful structure the size and shape of an almond. Talk about powerful things coming in small packages!

It's constantly on alert to the needs of basic survival and emotional reactions to our life experiences. An interesting finding, given that women are considered the more emotional of the genders, is that the amygdala is often *larger* in the male brain.

In addition to processing emotions, the amygdala also determines which memories are stored and where they are kept in our brains.

According to Daniel Goleman, the amygdala reacts before any possible direction from the neocortex can be received. He suggests that our emotions make us pay attention *right now*. If you've ever heard of the "fight or flight" response to an event, the little "almond" is where that powerful reaction originates.

When we face what Goleman has coined "amygdala hijacking," self control is very important. Although the "hijackings" often produce negative responses and reactions, these can have opposite outcomes. For example, hearty laughter in response to a joke can trigger a switch to true joy.

We can learn to control our amygdala by using humor, empathy or other appropriate tools to control an unpleasant or challenging situation. This is helpful for people who might experience "anxiety attacks" for instance.

Sherry Collier suggests using the six-second-rule. By taking six deep breaths, you can identify the stimulus and keep your cortex involved to control the amygdala. This method of controlling emotional fear can be very helpful in moving us forward and embracing change.

After the situation is over, rethinking the triggers will help shift the focus the *next* time from a negative response to a positive one. Meditation and mindfulness play a transformative role in amygdala responses by slowing down and calming the mind. This process allows for the all-important "being in the moment." It is also appropriate to express gratitude for a deeper understanding of how a positive response can keep us focused.

We can talk to the brain and ask the amygdala, the brain's worry center, to calm down. *What are your fears? What angers you?* How do we exchange these reactions for positive responses and feelings?

Using the **XXX *Change*** system presented in Session Six, we will learn to exchange worry, anger and fear for positive emotions of peace, love, trust and faith.

In the 1950s, Reuven Feuerstein claimed that the brain is plastic and modifiable at any age. More recently that theory was supported by Dr. Richard Restak, who wrote, "...your brain never loses the power to transform itself based on experiences."

Therefore, our brain is a lifetime work in progress that retains plasticity and the capacity for change, as long as we are alive and engaged with intention, attention, and constant repetition.

You've acquired a lot of powerful information in this session! So, now that you know how the brain is set up and connected to the rest of your body, let's use "The Brain Scan" meditation to integrate and activate the different parts of your wonderful aging brain!

The Brain Scan

The cortex organizes, plans and dreams
The new outer layer of our brain in this scheme.
The limbic system allows us to feel—
Our emotional center deep and real.
Breathe into feelings- become aware
The amygdala is also located here—
Turn the volume down, reduce anger and fear!
The anterior cingulate, the bridge between
The cortex and limbic—dreams and feelings.
The right and left sides integrate: lyrical, logical,
curvy and straight.
Temporal, parietal, occipital lobes allow the senses
to flourish and grow—
Turn up the volume from back to front as creativity
begins to flow.
Memories fire through the brain
Ending in the cortex where they remain.
From back to front, short to long-term to stay.
Neurotransmitters bathe the brain—
Feel rewards, focus and gains.
Feeling the divine in our brain,
In all parts as we meditate and pray,
Whatever we focus on, is displayed
As this incredible organ evolves day by day!

Using the tools of the Multi-Modal Method (MMM): music, movement, manual motion (sign language), mindful meditation, and creative visualization, the brain can form *new* neural pathways. Our experience in many years of using these modalities has produced a realization that changes in the brain can be positive, cumulative and unlimited. We can improve ourselves in a myriad of ways, leading to greater creativity, elevation of consciousness, feelings of unity, joy and trust.

The MMM practice is highly useful in promoting overall health, happiness and well being while our brain is being transformed on the physical, cognitive, social/emotional and spiritual level. This is the goal of the Onto the Next initiative—to let go of past limitations and embrace revitalizing change for the sake of holistic wellness.

Our intent is to offer a variety of joyful, effective, easy to use and inspirational tools to support this goal. When utilized daily with intention, attention, and repetition, these tools will help to rewire the brain and dramatically minimize many of the debilitating aspects associated with dementia and Alzheimer's.

II

Session Two: The Multi-Modal Method (MMM)

*The most beautiful and most profound
experience is the sensation of the mystical. It is
the power of all true science. He to whom this
emotion is a stranger, who can no longer
wonder and stand rapt in awe, is as good as
dead.*
Albert Einstein

Singing, dancing and gesture (sign
language) were forms of communication
long before language, literacy and scientific
study.

For centuries, in every culture, these
modalities were used. Labeled preverbal, these
methods are part of our biology and the
foundation of language as we know it today. As a
speech-language pathologist, The Multi-Modal
Method (MMM), music, movement, manual
motion or sign language and meditation, became

the way for Linda to tap into the more creative, authentic aspects of children as they learned language and literacy skills. Using these pre-verbal methods allowed new information and learning to be integrated and absorbed by the brain and the entire body.

Well, why wouldn't it work just as well in aging adults? As a professional in the domain of language, and as a caregiver for an aging parent with dementia, Linda was interested in minimizing the risks of dementia and Alzheimer's. And, for good reason.

Current statistics show us that one out of eight adults age 65 and older has dementia, and nearly one-half of those over age 85 have Alzheimer's disease. Women are four times more likely than men to get Alzheimer's and other dementias. The number of Americans with Alzheimer's and other dementias will grow each year as the proportion of the U.S. population over 65 continues to increase. According to the Alzheimer's Association (www.alz.org) currently 5.6 million Americans have Alzheimer's disease. By 2050, that number is expected to triple. In the next twenty years, it is expected that Alzheimer's will affect one out of every four Americans. The Alzheimer's Foundation reports that this number will not only escalate rapidly in the future as Baby Boomers age, but Alzheimer's is the fifth leading cause of death in individuals over age 65 here in the U.S.

Though the studies for causes and treatments are not conclusive at this time, it has been determined that as of 2012, cognitive decline can begin as early as age forty-five, when in 2007, it was thought that sixty was the minimum age for onset.

Understanding when the onset begins is important because interventions are far more effective when cognitive decline is first experienced, as indicated in an editorial by Francine Grodstein of Brigham and Women's Hospital in Boston, Massachusetts, United States.

So, if that is true, and there is enough research in agreement to support that theory, it makes perfect sense to develop a program that can be used and enjoyed by people of any age, but especially those who are approaching midlife, even in their early forties.

The goal of creating a comprehensive program is to utilize a significant amount of the brain, mind, body and spirit to support the whole individual. When we use the MMM, it taps into these preverbal modalities and utilizes tools to help us get in touch with our deeper, inner, creative selves. It allows the brain to *integrate* and *activate* in innovative ways.

The use of music, movement and manual motion (sign language), meditation and visualization, allows for a more complete balance of the right and left hemispheres of the brain. These techniques allow for the cortex and limbic system as well as the back and front lobes of the brain to collaborate. The entire brain, and thus the entire body, is utilized. We awaken our mind and whole brain to new and exciting thoughts, concepts and ways to promote change. Remember, change is "neuroplasticity"—the key to the brain remaining resilient and strong!

The risks of dementia and Alzheimer's can be diminished as we learn greater focus, attention, mindfulness, memory and processing skills. We can find life less stressful and we become more motivated as our self-awareness grows. Creativity is sparked as the brain is more fully integrated and engaged.

What does that look like? We experience calm, peace, trust, and joy when we feel confident, enthusiastic, passionate and positive. Engaging in this simple process, allows us to become more authentic, healthier, happier versions of ourselves. This is self-actualization!

Earlier we said that brain evolution does not end in our early twenties. That means that our brains evolve as we become more observant, conscious and accountable for our thoughts. We have the power as human beings to "retrain" our brains and develop them into new and exciting *minds*. Attention, repetition and intention, cognitive, physical, social-emotional and spiritual health and vitality are gently brought into balance as we learn new focus.

As intellect and spirit are tapped into, learning becomes rewarding, inspirational and exciting. Being observant, accountable, and present awakens this new potential.

New Brain Transforming Tools: The MMM
Music

Music predates modern culture by millions of years and has the ability to stimulate deep, primitive parts of the brain. Music is recognized by our brain's limbic system which is also the center of our emotional make-up. In fact, music changes our brain in profound ways. It can alter our moods, evoke feelings of love, beauty, and truth, as well as sorrow.

Music prepares us for change. It can deepen an emotional experience, enhance auditory and visual processing, and according to Dr. Andrew Newberg, author of *How God Changes Your Brain,* can improve attention and emotional processing. Newberg describes music as reducing stress while simultaneously enhancing memory. Studies show that singing a mantra (a repetitive phrase) can increase cognitive performance.

It is thought that music is actually encoded into our species, according to Daniel Amen, M.D., in *Change Your Brain, Change Your Life* and is associated with higher brain functioning.

When we utilize the term *music*, we are including singing, listening, and/or playing an instrument. Singing, chanting, humming and reciting poetry have additional healing effects on the temporal lobes and limbic system, asserts Dr. Amen.

Because of its plasticity, the brain stimulated by music can be more complex, healthier, and better functioning. Rhythm and melody bolster creativity, reduce stress, strengthen families, communities and connect us to our cultural heritage, says Don Campbell, in *The Mozart Effect*.

In addition, Dr. Oliver Sacks, neurologist and author of many books, speaks of Emmanuel Kant's philosophy of *music as a quickening art*. "Music helps memory as it restores people to themselves," says Sacks. He speaks of music as an aid to reacquiring one's identity as it animates, organizes and restores. According to Sacks, "...music imprints itself on the brain deeper than any other human experience."

In over seventy-five years of our combined experience, utilizing music in the learning process with children and adults, we have observed and noted the bonding that takes place between human beings when music is associated with an experience. Greats in the field of education such as Jean Piaget, Maria Montessori, Rudolph Steiner, Howard Gardner, and Friedrich Froebel, found music to be an important foundation to intellect, mathematical reasoning, creativity, and emotional/spiritual development. Music facilitates improved communication skills and can bring a sense of joy, gratitude and the feeling of well-being. Simply stated, music rewires the brain.

Lullabies are universal. They have the same impact whether sung or hummed. Scientists have strong reasons to suspect that Neanderthals, though they had no actual language as we know it today, communicated through music. Mark Jude Tramo, a neuroscientist/neurologist from Harvard Medical School, describes communicating emotions and ideas with grunts, groans and chants before enunciating complex ideas like the ones we're sharing now.

Matthew Fox, in his book, *Creativity*, quotes Hildegard of Bingen as describing, "...all atoms in the universe as busy vibrating and making music." She speaks of the first chakra or the "root chakra," which is the first energy center. This chakra connects us to all vibrations where universal sound is picked up.

"In the beginning was the sound." Chakras are the energy centers in our body through which energy flows. There are seven energy centers.

Recently, music was implemented in regular rehabilitative therapy to assist Gabrielle Giffords, the three-term congresswoman from

Arizona, who was tragically shot in the head in 2011. The bullet passed through her brain and then exited, causing significant damage. Music has helped her to learn to articulate words and express her thoughts.

Linda's mother Flo, who is now 94, has lost most of her ability to communicate with language. Her impairment is related to memory, attention span, problem solving and language. When Flo listens to music and sings, she is transformed. This becomes her new mode of communication. She remembers many of the songs she sang as a kindergarten teacher, mother, poet and songwriter. Music is now her most vital form of communication. She often sits in her rocking chair and hums. This relaxes her and allows her to be happy! Currently, Linda and her mother spend their time together singing, laughing and enjoying each other's company. The MMM allows Linda and her mother to communicate more than Linda ever thought possible

Gretchen's father, now in the early stages of dementia at age 89, responds to music when nothing else seems to work. Music, especially from the Big Band era, playing on the piano, radio, portable media player or stereo system brings joy to his face and a general calmness to his spirit. His memory is restored and he can "sing that song in one note." Recovering the lyrics, song title, and musician from the Big

Band era of the thirties and forties, music has rewired and engaged huge areas of his brain. Music and movement **are** the power switches to his brain.

Manual Motion (sign language)

Manual motion or sign language is another essential modality that empowers the brain to change. Sign language arrives into our mind through our eyes instead of our ears, as patterns in space rather than pitch.

Sign language is stored in the left side of the brain for most individuals, but in a separate place from oral language. Learning sign language is like learning a second language. It supports our communication and when used in conjunction with oral language can function as an important back-up system to help us remember, retrieve and process information.

Because of the visual and kinesthetic components, sign language activates both hemispheres of our brain and enhances the cognitive domain. Using sign language increases vocabulary, creating more connections to specific information. In our seminars, we use *signs* from ASL (American Sign Language). We do not use the *grammar* of ASL. The importance for our program, and the MMM, is that the practice of signing is key to neuroplasticity as it relates to healthy rewiring of the brain.

Retired Professor Marilyn Daniels, PhD., (Penn State) conducted extensive research with hearing children, using American Sign Language as a support for learning language and literacy. What she concluded was that learning sign language can make us smarter! Introducing sign language to support language and literacy with children and educators has also shown us positive changes in the childrens' confidence, self esteem and intelligence.

A day of signing allows for expanded communication skills and joyful feelings with a positive outlook. Finger spelling a name is a very helpful way to enhance our ability to remember and retrieve a person's name. When Linda meets new people, she always finger spells their names.

Mindful Meditation and Awareness

Meditation means "to plan in the mind," according to the American Heritage Dictionary. Neuroscience research is finding that meditation is linked to a myriad of measurable physical changes in the brain.

After two weeks of meditation practice, there is an increase in signaling connections in the brain, called "axonal density," as well as an increase in *myelin* (a white fatty tissue) around the axons in the region of the brain where motivation resides.

Meditation retrains our brains by "molding and shaping" to install the changes we want, creating a synchronization of the two hemispheres of the brain. Imagine two people in a dance class. They each dance alone. But dancing together, to create a magical, powerful dance, takes practice and training.

Meditation is an invitation to wake up and transform. *It does not make your mind blank.* It plays a role in supporting plasticity. It is integrative and increases brain signaling connections. Dr. Richard Davidson, at the University of Wisconsin-Madison, has conducted studies with Tibetan monks and lay practitioners who meditate regularly. MRI scans revealed significant changes to activity in the left and right regions of their brains. Davidson says, "We can take advantage of our brain's plasticity and train it to enhance compassion, kindness, and love, through mindful meditation."

In order to derive the powerful and life-changing benefits of meditation, one need not attend a retreat for days or weeks to meditate continually. Simply decide with intention to awaken in the morning and allow 12-20 minutes for the practice of meditation. You will be thrilled and amazed at how this will help to focus and relax your busy mind for the coming day.

There are numerous meditative practices available to those who wish to explore different methods. Transcendental Meditation is a very simple, easy-to-use and effective meditation. Simple Breathing Meditation, observing one's in-and-out breath while sitting quietly, is another time-proven practice. It's not the specific *type* of meditation that's important. What's important is the intention and practice of doing *some* form of meditation.

Mindfulness means experiencing life as it unfolds, moment to moment. The four components of *mindfulness* are: attention, body awareness, emotional regulation, and a sense of self. Taking our lives off society's imposed autopilot to become sensitive to the nuances of everyday experience is what mindfulness is about.

Daniel Siegel, M.D., in *The Mindful Brain*, speaks of reflecting on the mind and making conscious choices. Whatever we focus on directly shapes our mind and our brain. When we pay attention to the present moment, a special form of awareness is created. This awareness says Siegel, helps to regulate emotions, improve patterns of thinking, reduce negativity, lower stress, increase the immune response, and boost our physical well-being.

We are able to be here with more compassion and a greater ability to empathize. With so much suffering in every society today, people who can be in a mindful place will add to the kindness and consciousness of the world. Mindfulness helps us attune to others: it is doing one thing at a time. It is **not** multi tasking!

Alignment

We are here to align
Body, soul, spirit, mind.
Be aware of yourself
And your neighbor on each side.
Here as one
Connected from within—
Focus, relax and smile,
As we align
Body, soul, spirit, mind.

As we begin our efforts to strengthen our awareness, we employ a practice called *alignment*. Alignment allows us to focus on the changes we desire in our lives, our attitudes, and our spirits.

We begin by sitting quietly and comfortably with eyes closed. Gently and slowly breathe in a relaxed manner. Our focus is on our *intention*. This means that we are conscious of our desire to bring about a positive and intentional change in how we approach our daily life. By setting an intention, we empower our mind, body, spirit and soul toward alignment.

This tool opens our mind and allows us to focus on greater potential for fulfillment in our lives. It is helpful to be grateful for our lives. This gives us the ability to live in the present instead of dwelling on the past which we cannot change, or the future for which we don't have a crystal ball.

There are no mistakes in how we perform alignment. If you are home with your partner, loved one, or pet, you may gently place your hand on their back as you share this alignment process. This can be done in silence or out loud. If you live alone and have no pets, you can still embrace this alignment practice effectively.

Repeating this daily, preferably first thing in the morning, will reinforce a positive intention and healthy outlook for the coming day.

Saa Taa Naa Maa Meditation

During the first segment of our seminars, we introduce a spoken and gestural meditation from traditional Kundalini Yoga, *Saa Taa Naa Maa.* These represent the primal sounds of the Universe which help to balance both hemispheres of the brain and can be a simple and effective catalyst for change.

Finger positions are integrated along with the chanting of the sounds. Using both hands at the same time, *Saa* (index finger to thumb), *Taa* (middle finger to thumb), *Naa* (ring finger to thumb) and *Maa* (pinky to thumb). Continue this meditation exercise for 10 minutes silently. Relax and become aware of mental processes. Let them flow through your mind. Use this mantra each day for 12 minutes. For the last 2 minutes, chant the mantra out loud continuing to use finger positions. This daily 12-minute practice allows for greater focus and relaxation during the day.

When finished, put your hands together in prayer position in front of you, tapping each finger individually and sit quietly for another minute before embarking on your day!

According to Dr. Andrew Newberg, psychiatrist and neuroscience researcher, many measurable, positive changes take place in the brain when this mantra is used. Newberg notes activity in the pre-frontal cortex, which supports memory, cognition, focus, planning, dreaming and imagining.

In addition, the part of the brain known as the *anterior cingulate*, which regulates emotions, moods and motivation is affected. The amygdala changes, allowing for a reduction of stress, depression, anger and anxiety.

Finally, the limbic system activates compassion and empathy. We are more relaxed, orderly and productive. We can set an intention for the frontal lobes and begin to see changes. Cognitive health and vitality are supported giving us greater clarity and consciousness.

35

The movement of the fingers affects the cerebellum which is involved with motor coordination. This mantra, when practiced daily, can help slow dementia, Alzheimer's disease and the aging process overall.

Yoga and Breathing

Another effective practice to enhance focus and relaxation is known as *yoga*. It not only includes physical movements but also active attention or mindfulness. One of the main purposes of yoga is to retrain the brain to stop the automatic triggering of the stress response.

Yoga involves the process of focusing one's attention on the present moment while simultaneously calming the mind with a sustained intention of this focus.

Yoga has the capacity to help rewire our brains and help our memory grow sharper and stronger in just twenty minutes per day. Yoga boosts levels of the brain chemical GABA, which helps to promote calmness.

Breathing is free, simple, easy and always accessible. Breathing intentionally for relaxation is a powerful adjunct to other practices that support relaxation. Dr. Herbert Benson, cardiologist and founder of the Benson-Henry Institute for Mind Body Medicine of Harvard University, has many techniques for relaxation.

A popular relaxation breathing exercise is known as 4-7-8. Dr. Andrew Weil recommends this technique in his *Guide to Living Longer and Better* (Spring 2014 Edition 41).

- ♥ Place the tip of your tongue against the ridge behind your upper front teeth.
- ♥ Exhale completely through your mouth making a *whoosh* sound. Close your mouth and inhale quietly through your nose to a count of *4* in your mind.
- ♥ Next, hold your breath for a count of *7*.
- ♥ Then exhale completely through your mouth making a *whoosh* sound to a count of 8. This is one complete breath cycle.
- ♥ Repeat this 3 more times for a total of 4 cycles.

This practice, when completed daily, is a valuable tool to reduce stress and elevate one's mood.

Cross Lateralization

Movements such as body tapping, stretching, and arm and leg crossovers, encourage both hemispheres of the brain to "talk" to each other. This is also known as "*cross lateralization.*"

The concept of cross motor activities for the brain and body are powerful tools to assist with left and right side integration. These cross lateralization or mid-line movements activate the speech and language centers of the brain, both expressively and receptively. Some mid-line activities have the ability to increase brain-body coordination.

Take It Easy

Take it easy
Nice and slow
Then you'll know
Which way to go
Going easy
You will find
Helps to focus
And relax your mind

As you say this meditation, use your index finger as a guide, beginning with your right hand to trace the outline of a figure 8 on its side. Slowly and gently follow this figure 8 pattern. At the end of the meditation switch hands to the left and do it again. It is important to make the pattern wide enough to work easily. Therefore go approximately two feet wide from end to end. You can do it again if you so desire, using both hands simultaneously.

Just a reminder: keep reciting the meditation as you do the figure 8s.

The Brainy Walk

In order to assist you with further mid-line crossing (cross lateralization), refer to Linda Stoler's CD, *Brainysounds*. The song titled, *the Brainy Walk* was created to engage in cross lateralization.

Linda began doing her cross lateralization walk some fifteen years ago. She discovered it while walking her dog down a country road in Vermont. With the dog's leash tied around her waist, she walked hands free, swinging her arms from right to left past her mid-line.

She synchronized this movement with her right arm crossing over her left knee and her left arm crossing over her right knee. Upon her return home, she noticed a distinct clarity and flow to her writing. She regularly walks with her dog in this fashion. Cross-country skiing and crawling like a young child create the same cross lateralization movements. Because of this practice, Linda wrote the "Brainy Walk." A soon-to-be-released DVD will demonstrate this and other exercises, to transform your aging brain.

Yawning

Yawning is a very good exercise to strengthen circulation to the brain. In fact, yawning increases brain activity to keep us alert. It stimulates and relaxes the entire body. You should cover a yawn, but don't inhibit the relaxed expression of it. Yawning further expands the lung capacity by allowing for deeper breathing. You can even pretend to yawn, thereby creating the same effects that a true yawn brings about. The most recent research on yawning suggests that yawning exists to cool down the brain.

Smiling

Smiling is more important than laughter. Smiling reduces stress. It lowers the heart rate. Smiling releases endorphins that counteract and diminish stress hormones. It lifts your mood, increases productivity, and encourages trust and empathy. Smiling increases attention, lessens pain, and makes us more attractive. Smiling is contagious.

Nhat Hanh, a Zen Buddhist monk, and author of *Peace is Every Step:The Path of Mindfulness in Everyday Life,* and *The Miracle of Mindfulness* says, "Smiling is very important. If we are not able to smile, then the world will not have peace. It is with our capacity of smiling, breathing and being peace that we can make peace."

Around 50 % of the people you smile at will return the smile. People who smile sincerely have stronger immune systems, and studies have proven that they can live approximately seven years longer than the group who did not employ the conscious act of smiling at others. Smiling can also be a natural face lift since it can make us look significantly younger!

Tapping

Emotional Freedom Techniques, known as EFT or "tapping," uses the fingers to tap on various *meridian points* of the body. Science, including studies done at the Mayo Clinic in New York, verify that the body contains 12 energy channels which are called *meridians*. Tapping is sometimes referred to as "emotional acupuncture without needles." This practice allows for an exchange of negative thoughts for positive ones.

For example, someone experiencing fear might want to experience confidence instead. That might sound like this: "I feel afraid, yet I love and accept myself for who I am." The following meridian points should be gently tapped with finger tips 5-7 times at the following locations:

- ♥ Start of the eyebrow near the bridge of the nose
- ♥ Side of the eye near the temple
- ♥ Under the eye
- ♥ Under the nose
- ♥ The crease between the chin and lip
- ♥ The collar bone
- ♥ Underneath the arm
- ♥ Top of the head

Tapping and the Thymus Gland

"The thymus gland serves as the link between mind and body. It is the first organ to be affected by mental attitudes and stress. Hence, activation and stimulation of the thymus is an essential, primary foundation of achieving and maintaining positive health." This observation was published by Dr. John Diamond, author of *Your Body Doesn't Lie*, a book that essentially demonstrates the impact that positive and negative thoughts have upon our physical body.

The thymus gland is largest when we are infants and shrinks as we age. It is a gland important for production of *T-cells* which are vital to a healthy immune system.

The thymus is involved with the flow of lymph throughout the body. It monitors and regulates energy flow and helps to instantaneously correct imbalances of body energy. Tapping the thymus, which is located below the collar bone at the center top of the sternum, is essential to achieving and maintaining positive health.

Metacognition

The process of *metacognition* allows us to become more mindful, observant and thus accountable for our thoughts and feelings. As we become more mindful and observe our thoughts, we can begin to rewire our brain and body to become more conscious. In this awakened place, we look inward and acknowledge the wisdom we have acquired through the years. We begin to live in the present, letting go of the past and trusting the future.

In his book *Mindsight*, Dr. Daniel Siegel discusses internal equilibrium which is crucial to cognitive wellness. The process of paying attention to the present moment, without being judgmental, allows neural firing which leads to the production of proteins that allow new connections to be made among neurons.

This biological process promotes health, brain hygiene and an integration of consciousness. In the Zen Buddhist tradition, avoiding the extremes of elation and despair is considered an essential component of a balanced and holistic life.

Focus and Attention

As human beings, we have the natural ability to focus on *anything*. Brain cells are continually reorganized by our thoughts and experiences. What we think about and where we focus our attention is what we become, neurologically speaking.

"Scanning the landscape and choosing what to focus on and what to leave in the background is one of our greatest gifts," wrote Daniel Goleman. These skills are essential to our ability to realize our potential as creative human beings. As Goleman discusses in his book, *The Hidden Driver of Excellence,* a well-lived life demands that we be nimble in three kinds of focus: *inner, other* and *outer.*

Inner focus attunes us to our intuitions and guiding values. *Other* focus supports our connections to the people in our lives. *Outer* focus lets us navigate the larger world.

Goleman also discusses the basics of *attention,* the cognitive muscle that allows us to follow a story, see a task through to completion, to learn, or to create.

A failure to focus leaves us in a state of *lack of attention* to the task at hand. This will often leave us feeling just a bit unsettled or uneasy, though we might not understand exactly why.

Again, we are reminded of the importance of being *in the moment* as a component of mindfulness and our innate ability to be present. In order to maintain focus and attention it is important to be mindful of what we are *actually* focusing on. Therefore, when we pay attention to what we are focusing on, we are strengthening the "focus muscle."

Psychiatrist Dr. Daniel Seigel describes the wiring that links both attuning to ourselves and others as a "resonance circuit" that is strengthened when we practice mindfulness. Seigel emphasizes that mindfulness strengthens critical brain connections and, that through practicing awareness, we can become less impulsive.

When we are focused and mindful, we are able to observe our mental processes rather than be overwhelmed by them. This is another powerful tool not only in the transformation of our aging brains, but in maintaining good mental health at any age.

Visualization

If you can see it, you can reach it.
Myles Abe Peterson

Visualization allows us to create pictures in our mind. With a focus on positive images, we establish healthy brain patterns.

A Harvard University study that clearly demonstrates the value of visualization was named, *The Piano Study*. The study involved three selected groups of participants. The outcome of the study revealed and documented the awareness of structural changes to the brain, and strongly suggested that if we can *imagine* it, we can *create* it, and the physical changes will be apparent in the brain.

One group was charged with actually practicing exercises on a real piano. A second group was charged with visualizing playing the exercises, but was not allowed to play an actual piano. Both groups were tested to establish their baseline brain maps.

At the end of the testing period, the group that had *visualized* playing the piano exercises exhibited the same brain changes as the group who had *actually* played the piece. A third group did nothing and demonstrated no brain changes. Visualization is so powerful that the brain does not distinguish between what we are actually doing and what we visualize!

Dr. Herbert Benson, Harvard Medical School, demonstrated that a positive visualization of a healthy body can actually change the expression of the genes.

While working with Harvard Medical School to uncover the connection between elevated blood pressure on patients without any history of blood pressure problems, he was asked to work with a group that practiced *intentional meditation*. What he discovered was that there indeed was a documentable mind-body connection.

Further study revealed that many patients diagnosed with high blood pressure, anxiety, depression, infertility, insomnia, and other phobias and pain that included backaches and headaches, were able to improve their health because of neuroplasticity that resulted from changing their thought patterns and attitudes.

Okay–so what does that mean for us? We should be singing, dancing and shouting for joy! It's time to imagine what we want to do with the rest of our lives. Who will we visualize ourselves to be tomorrow and into the future? What were we put here on earth to do? What seeds were planted when we were born? What are our gifts and talents? What do we envision ourselves doing that is our bliss? What can we do that erases the boundaries? What is our purpose, our passion? How can we successfully re-imagine and revitalize our lives?

If you listen to the stories of successful people, many of them will refer to childhood dreams that allowed them to visualize and believe they could become who they imagined. It is never too late. Grandma Moses began painting at age 90—and Colonel Sanders, founder of the Kentucky Fried Chicken Corporation, started that business at the age of 65!

Movement/Dance

The way we move our bodies relates to the way we feel about ourselves. Practically the entire brain contributes to body movements. Planned movements start in the motor cortex, where signals travel to twenty-million nerve fibers.

In dancing, many parts of the brain act together to turn a body's motion from discrete movements into fluid, physical art form. We need physical awareness to dance. A cluster of brain cells called the *basal ganglia* plan movement while the *cerebellum* takes sensory input from our limbs and processes signals in the cortex to create smooth, flowing motion.

Movement and dance strengthen memory, motor skills, cognition, organization, language and creativity. Dance and movement improve rhythm and timing and are critical to planning and sequencing actions and thoughts. In addition, dancing brings out the joy inside us. In a study over a twenty-one year period by the Albert Einstein College of Medicine in New York City, a surprising outcome was revealed. Almost none of the typical physical activities appeared to offer any protection against dementia *except* frequent dancing.

We say dancing is the best form of exercise!

Gretchen grew up dancing on Sunday mornings with her dad, a dance instructor in

Boston after World War II. She continues to enjoy dancing no matter where she hears music. And, we can back up our declaration with a lot of evidence. For example, in October 2013, "Psychology Today" published the results of two studies done at the University of California.

"Through regular aerobic training that incorporates some type of dance at least once a week, anyone can maximize his or her brain function."

Dr. Daniel Wolpert of Cambridge and Oxford is a medical doctor who continued on into neuroscience where he is regarded as a leading researcher on human motor control. He claims, "The brain creates the grace and agility of human motion."

Linda became an aerobics instructor, at nearly 50 years old. She was concerned about her ability to remember the numerous dance routines required. She soon realized to her delight, that not only did she remember the moves, but that it was effortless. The brain and body have the ability to remember and retrieve physical movements, even at 50 and beyond!

III

Session Three: Right and Left Hemispheres

We all need a balanced, integrated brain.
Jill Bolte-Taylor

The human brain is divided into right and left *hemispheres.* Although it is understood that each half of the brain has different responsibilities, it is acknowledged that both hemispheres of the brain share some responsibilities for different functions.

The right brain thinks mostly in pictures, is more non-verbal, learns *kinesthetically* through movement, and is more peaceful. It is emotional, learns through the senses and allows us to feel a connection to all others. Les Fehmi, PhD, in *The Open-Focus Brain*, mentions that the right brain is better equipped to perceive facial signals, coordinate singing, comprehend music, read body language, and carry out tasks such as throwing a ball or riding a bike.

51

The right brain, according to Fehmi, takes in more of the big picture and context in both a literal and metaphorical sense. It sees many things simultaneously rather than sequentially. This is called *parallel processing*. It perceives a whole face rather than one feature at a time. Familiarity and recognition are right brain functions.

The left brain is more linear, logical, rational, and mathematical. It has greater responsibility for serial processing, details, and categories. It is more organized, thinking about the past and the future. It is the dominant hemisphere in our culture. The left hemisphere, with its emphasis on language, can recognize a song's words but has no memory for its melody. We all tend to have a dominant hemisphere.

Right-brained individuals can be more creative with a broader, big-picture outlook. Fehmi states that they are less concerned about details such as time and deadlines and balancing their checkbook; for example, artists, performers, and those dealing with imagination and invention are more inclined to be right-brained.

It's estimated that two thirds of American society is left-brain dominant. Many occupations and most males, says Fehmi, favor left brain function. The United States educational system, government, military, and workplaces, are presently left-brain biased. These institutions are concerned with written language, time, deadlines, serial processing and testing. Left-brain dominance is currently rewarded in our society.

In his book, *A Whole New Mind*, Daniel Pink discusses the fact that we are presently moving into a new age: *the Conceptual Age*. He speaks of our societal evolution from agriculture to industry; to the information age; and finally now, to the *conceptual* age. We are moving from farm to factory to knowledge and finally to creativity and care-partnering. These are qualities that will require new ways of thinking and being—along with new careers.

Counseling, nursing, health, art and design, as well as education, will take over in importance. At best, there will be a blending and support of more whole-brain initiatives and attributes.

In his book, Pink's six fundamental right-brain directed aptitudes are explained: *design, story, symphony, empathy, play*, and *meaning*.

Design refers to something beautifully designed or emotionally engaging rather than just functional.

Story involves being able to tell a story for persuasion and communication and not just for the sake of argument.

Symphony is all about seeing the big picture and not just analyzing the small pieces. People with this attribute are who Pink has labeled, "boundary-crossers." Pink's definition of boundary-crossers are those individuals who have lived what he calls "hyphenated lives; individuals who have a wide background and have crossed multiple boundaries."

Empathy is essential for people and organizations to thrive. Technology simply does not have the ability to empathize or build relationships.

Play and its value cannot be highlighted enough. From the field of early childhood education, we know how critical play is to a child's understanding of the world. Laughter, humor, and joy are essential.

Meaning is all about pursuing significant desires, purpose, and spiritual fulfillment. According to Pink, "These six aptitudes will guide our lives and shape our world."

Pink, along with many others, believes that our current educational system in the U.S. still prepares our children primarily for the world of the past, rather than for possible worlds of the future.

Our society will need more people who can make connections between disparate information and innovation like storytellers, caregivers, designers, meaning-makers, inventors, creators, artists, and big picture thinkers. The time is right for societal and cultural changes.

By using more of the whole brain, we can be instrumental in shaping a profound paradigm shift. *This is likely to influence our evolution.* When we work on cross-lateralization, using both sides of the brain, we will be more fully integrating the right and left hemispheres providing greater balance, clearer thought and strong forward movement.

Jill Bolte-Taylor, a neuroanatomist at Harvard University, had a major stroke at the age of thirty-seven. In her book, *My Stroke of Insight*, she discusses how after her left-brain stroke, she lived mostly in her right brain, a non-confrontational freeform world of kinesthetic, visual experiences. Bolte-Taylor lectures now on the importance of right brain experience and balancing both sides of the brain.

Bolte-Taylor has become a strong spokesperson for the power of neuroplasticity and integration of the brain.

IV

Session Four: Universal Energy

Nothing in the natural order of the universe is random. Our existence is not mere luck. Everything physical in life is not solid matter, it's all energy! Albert Einstein

D r. Joe Dispenza, in his book, *Breaking the Habit of Being Yourself*, explores the idea that we each have a distinct energy pattern or signature. It is postulated that we are made up of these particles that actually are interconnected through time and space. A Universal Intelligence or Infinite Mind resides in all matter and continually provides the properties and actions for all.

For centuries, human historical observation and deductive reasoning have led to the universal belief (though there are many cultural differences in explanation) that there is an order and intelligence to the entire universe. This argument was first used by Greek philosopher

Anaxagoras, 450 B.C., to transform chaos into order. Researchers are considering the possibility that intelligence exists in each of our cells and that it gives its essence to everything and is completely receptive and malleable in response to our attention and intention.

Our brain is the center of everything we do and everything we are. This incredible organ is the part of our living self that allows us the emotions of connection, joy, peace, love, compassion, empathy and mindfulness. Many believe that by connecting to our higher-self, we access the Higher Intelligence. This spiritual aspect of humanity provides an unlimited well from which we can draw. Dispenza says that when we resonate with this Intelligence, we become the elevated power that transcends the past, heals the present, and opens doors to the future. We may ask this Intelligence for assistance.

If we seek joy, we will not find it in a place of suffering. So, if joy is not to be occasional or accidental, we will only find it if we can access that place within us where it resides. John Lennon and Paul McCartney wrote the Beatles' hit, *The End* and the lyrics demonstrate this point:

> *And in the end—the love you take*
> *Is equal to the love— you make.*

What we put out is what we receive, as the outer world reflects our inner reality. It is a counterproductive pursuit to be focused on worry, to be anxious or doubtful. Optimism has terrific benefits. Believe in the best possible outcome, surrender, and be thankful.

Gratitude is a key element that allows us to live our lives in the present. This consciousness gives us *mindful* awareness of who we are and what we are thinking and feeling. We can create an event to correspond to whatever the mind puts into the energetic field. We can be responsible and aware of what we are thinking and putting out to this Intelligence. Visualization supports this awareness.

Dr. Valerie Hunt, a neurophysiologist and Professor Emeritus at UCLA, speaks about the human energy field from the study of bioenergetics. From a "Mu Room" at UCLA, a shielded room where electromagnetic energy can be altered, she explained the effects of the electromagnetism of air.

When the electromagnetic air was depleted, it produced tears and sadness but when the electromagnetic air was increased, clearer thinking resulted.

She calls this phenomenon, "human vibrations of consciousness." Perhaps this points to the centuries-old knowledge of the importance of *mindful* breathing to support this phenomenon.

V

Session Five: Unlearning and Obstacle Thinking

What you believe, is what you become. You become what you think.
Earl Nightingale

I learned that courage was not the absence of fear, but the triumph over it. The brave man is not he who does not feel afraid, but he who conquers that fear.
Nelson Mandela.

Many of us live with outdated and incorrect messages that play constantly in the background of our mind: *We aren't strong enough. We aren't tall enough. We aren't fast/smart/cool enough,* or, how about, *We're too old to learn new things.*

These thoughts often are about past regrets or future concerns. They take us away from the all important awareness of the present moment. We want to make the intentional choice to change our thinking and responses. *Metacognition,* as referred to earlier, is about becoming more observant and thus accountable for our thoughts and feelings. It's about staying in the present and being focused and intentional, every day and every way!

Metamemory is an important form of metacognition or *knowing* about memory. Since we've established that our thinking influences our health and events, we would certainly benefit from giving serious attention to our *own* thought processes.

For instance, to realize when we are thinking something that isn't positive or powerful, there is a way to stop that sort of thinking. But we have to be paying attention to what we're thinking in order to change it!

We've shown how the flow of thoughts sculpt the brain. If we change our thinking, which physiologically changes our brain, we can change our life! From this more awakened place we can also look inward and acknowledge the wisdom we have acquired through the years, keeping in mind that wisdom is acquired from our accumulated past experiences.

We reflect on our thoughts, feelings, and decisions and continually assess them. We maintain an ongoing commentary in the back of our mind, based on previous, "old messages." Fundamental to our sense of self is knowing who we truly are. MRIs taken by Fleming and his team at University College (London, 2010) evidenced that those who could assess their own thinking had more grey matter in the prefrontal cortex.

As we become more aware and get in touch with our thought processes, it is important to continuously monitor what we are thinking. How much of our thinking is controlled by negative thoughts? The *basal ganglia* and amygdala are responsible for thoughts of worry, fear and obsession. These powerful and counterproductive feelings and thoughts must be dealt with because they are significant obstacles to holistic wellness and joy as we age.

Louise Hay, author of the best-selling *Heal Your Body,* and president of Hay House, says, "The thoughts we choose to think are the tools we use to paint the canvas of our lives." The use of positive affirmations has been proven to be very powerful in healing of many types.

In his book, *Creativity,* Matthew Fox talks about obstacles people have to their creativity. Just imagine boulders that need to be rolled back so that we can be in touch with our essential, creative, magnificent selves.

Obstacle thinking takes the form of: *I can't do this because..., I am too old, tired, busy, etc., I don't have enough...time, money, energy, etc., I am too sad, angry, fearful, etc., I am afraid of dying, I am too shy, I am afraid of being alone, I am afraid of abandonment, I am afraid I won't be able to do anything.* The list can be endless.

According to Matthew Fox, the late M.C. Richards wrote, "We have to realize that a creative being lives within ourselves, whether we like it or not, and that we must get out of its way, for it will give us no peace until we do."

As we begin to become more aware, conscious, awake and present in the moment, we can begin to regulate and even change these old thought patterns and rewire our brains toward a more powerful way of thinking.

Many of history's recognized leaders reflected traits of elevated thinking: Mahatma Gandhi, Martin Luther King, Nelson Mandela, Jane Goodall, Margaret Mead and the Dalai Lama to name a few.

Love, compassion and community are components of positive thinking and renewal that move us toward a oneness with ourselves *and* with one another.

"The human brain is prewired for loving, spiritual resilience, and community welfare," says George Vaillant, M.D., Director of Harvard's Longitudinal Study of Adult Development.

Intentional affirmations are crucial to wellness and joy—and aging well. They stimulate changes in our brain and allow us to see ourselves in more positive and gratifying ways.

Session Six: XXX Change

The process of maturing is a very subtle one for the simple reason that we are both the molding material and steadily becoming our own molders.
Moshe Feldenkrais

We've learned that our brains can continue to learn new things even after the age of 21. We've learned that having fun, being positive, and learning to love and embrace every current moment is good for us mentally, physically and spiritually.

According to George Vaillant, M.D., as we mature in life, we move toward embracing the spiritual aspects of ourselves. We can live from a more elevated place of love, peace, compassion, empathy, joy, connection, fulfillment and abundance. This is our evolution. Continuously attaching ourselves to our feelings of fear, anger and sadness keeps us stuck in a place of mistrust and doubt.

Through neuroplasticity, we can learn a new way to exchange, or **XXX Change,** our negative feelings, thoughts and repetitive "tape loops." We can intentionally get off the emotional roller coaster and begin to acquire new empowering thoughts and messages. These positive, elevated thoughts and feelings will eventually replace feelings of fear and mistrust and bring forth trust and faith in our everyday living experience.

This process of rewiring our brain must be done *daily,* moment to moment, with attention, intention and constant repetition. Just like we would get our ingredients together before we prepare a meal, the **XXX Change** technique is a life sustaining practice.

So, here we go! When we have a negative feeling or thought, we must *visualize* three **X**'s over the word that defines the negative thought.

For example: visualize the word *FEAR*, and in your mind, place three **X**'s right over it. Then envision the word **CHANGE** stamped over the **X**'s.

Next, visualize the entire feeling of *fear* crumbling as a cracker would crumble in the hand of a child.

Step by step, this is how we can rewire our brain. Using the power of visualization, we begin to live in a freeing, peaceful and universal consciousness by taking our mind and brain there again and again through the **XXX Change** process.

Jeanne White, a close friend and career therapist, explains the **XXX Change** process in another way: "It's like bringing something back to Target. There is never a problem making a return. No questions asked, we simply don't need this anymore!"

We can learn to free ourselves from the negative feelings and trust fully with faith!

The **XXX Change** process is most effective when a "body scan" is done *first* to bring awareness to the brain and body. It establishes a deeper level of consciousness.

Play soothing, restful instrumental music to accompany this exercise. As each body part is mentioned, take a moment to be aware of it and visualize a healthy, properly functioning body part. With eyes closed, breathe deeply and welcome a sense of relaxation. Pause before moving on to the next body part. Allow approximately 5-8 minutes for the entire scan.

Body Scan

*Bring awareness to your head, as on your neck it sits
and rests.
Bring awareness to your brain, feel the connections
as they grow and change, rearrange.
Now to your eyes, let them see deep inside
And to your ears, tune them up-let them hear-
Your nose that smells, the aromas compel,
And now to your mouth, taste is what it's about.
Words articulated, lips, tongue and teeth...
Your larynx and breath from your lungs help you
speak.
Your upper torso houses your heart- shine a light,
heal each part.
All of your organs, each one in its place...
Work together in this glorious space-let them all
interface.
The beauty of your back, the strength of your spine,
Feel the healing at this time.
Of your lower torso be aware, hips and buttocks,
shine the light there.
Your arms and legs give your body a chance...
To help and serve, walk and dance, as your servants
they enhance.
Be aware of your knees, ankles and feet, as your toes
wiggle and make you complete.
Now be aware of the space surrounding you;
Let a light come shining through.
You are precious, healthy, and fine.
Smile and rejoice in your body at this time.
A perfect example—a divine design!*

To prepare your mind to visualize this powerful change, take a deep breath, and do the next meditation.

The *XXX Change* Meditation

Take the feelings you no longer need...
Fear, doubt, anger, greed.
XXX Change with a Higher Power, please.
XXX Change thoughts and feelings keeping you
from your dreams.
In a new way, XXX Change for love and faith,
And from this very elevated place
See yourself in this new space.

Take a deep breath, smile, and repeat this meditation. Then, remain in this place, feel the feelings of awe, beauty, love, excitement, joy, connection, and wonder!

Now that we are calm, peaceful and understand the power of our mind, we are ready for the life-changing next step! This is where we blast those negative thoughts out of existence and adopt and embrace the thoughts that will change our quality of life!

The XXX Change Mantra

XXX Change—
Crumble it up! Rearrange –
Surrender to a higher plane
Fear to faith – Rename
This is the way to rewire your brain!
Do it again and again and again . . . .

In addition to exchanging *Fear for Faith*, for example, you may also utilize the following exchanges as tools for rewiring your brain:

Sickness to Health
Scarcity to Abundance
Doubt to Confidence
Sadness to Joy
Pain to Love
Anger to Compassion
Worry to Trust
Trapped to Freedom
Insomnia to Sleep
Anxiety to Peace
Judgment to Acceptance

Memorize this mantra and make it portable. Think of it as a survival tool to attach to your belt and access easily whenever you feel stuck!

We surrender the old feeling to a Higher Power and **XXX *Change*** it for positive thoughts and empowered feelings. Letting go of a negative thought or feeling is perhaps one of the most difficult challenges we face, but the rewards are nothing short of amazing!

VII

Session Seven: The New Authentic You

In conjunction with **The Body Scan**, the **XXX Change Meditation** and the **Mantra**, the next step of your daily practice is to recite the meditation on the next page.

This works well when accompanied by instrumental music and is intended as a meditation to take us to a place where we use the visualization technique as a tool to help establish our new, authentic selves!

Remember how powerful visualization techniques are! Allow your mind to envision you in a new, different, healthier way, engaged in a life that supports self-actualization.

The New Authentic You

All of the wonders that make you complete
Visualize in your mind's eye to see.
Look at them now, see what belongs—
Paint a new picture, sing a new song.
What are you doing that you love to do?
Authentic passion with your voice that is true—
See yourself, let this embrace you.
Picture the beautiful things you can do,
All you came to earth to be—
Be that now, authentic and free.
Visualize yourself in your mind's eye to see.
There is a legacy you can leave,
Something significant you will be.

Now embrace gratitude as you visualize—
the New Authentic You!

This next exercise is a powerful affirmation!
Affirmations are compatible with the **XXX
Change** and are essential in supporting The
New Authentic You. Visualize looking at yourself
in the mirror and say the following out loud,
with feeling:

I Am

I am Faith

I am Health

I am Abundance

I am Confidence

I am Joy

I am Love

I am Forgiveness

I am Compassion

I am Trust

I am Peace

I am Unity

I am Freedom

I am Passion

I am Present in the Moment

Infinite Mind and A New Authentic You

Dr. Joe Dispenza, in his book, *Breaking the Habit of Being Yourself*, speaks of the mind in an elevated place as being "synchronized." These are the moments when a positive sense of trust, joy, and inspiration can take over. Dispenza speaks of a shift from a compartmentalized, over-focused, narrow-minded, "survival-mode" of being to a more open, relaxed, holistic, present and creative state.

Psychologist Donald Hebb of Canada is credited with Hebb's "law of firing" which states that when we do anything long enough, we begin to *know* how to do it.

"Neurons that fire together, wire together." With attention, intention and repetition, new neural networks will reflect new thoughts and feelings and uncover new ways of being. This result can be the beginning of The New Authentic You. From these practices, we can create a new reality. Remember, the more we practice something, the better we get at it.

Dispenza speaks of pictures in our mind which become vibrational blueprints of a new destiny. He mentions being creative and diverse in visualizing our new identity. "We must fall in love with the vision of who we are, rehearsing a new ideal self which can be memorized and brought forth consistently."

Richard Restak wrote, "Brain connections are like friendships. Those that are maintained will endure. Those neglected will disappear."

Our New Authentic being can be a healthier, more whole and joyful version of who we have been. The New Authentic You is more mindful, loving, aware, compassionate, empathetic, connected and vital.

Imagine, for example, that we have a contract with the *Infinite Mind* that was signed before we were born. That contract is to *fulfill our potential*—to be who we *truly* are! What are our passions? What gives us joy from the inside? What gifts ignite us? What do we see ourselves doing that we love to do? What is our bliss? What do we do that makes us lose track of time?

This is the contract that is longing to be fulfilled. We signed this contract before we took our first breath of air. Now it's time to complete it. Antonio Damasio, in *Looking for Spinoza*, says we should "actively seek joy."

George Vaillant, M.D., in his book, *Spiritual Evolution*, speaks of joy as contributing to flourishing.

The poem on page 80 can be used to reinforce peace while we are learning about our own blissful dreams and goals.

Rewire Your Aging Brain
"The New Authentic You"

Brain neurons to rewire

Old thoughts and feelings to retire

Sacred and divine

Dance, sing and sign

To visualize

Re-align

In perfect time

This grand design

Hope, love, awe, inspire

Intertwine

The sky's the limit

Time to fly!

THE SKY'S THE LIMIT – WHAT DO **YOU** DREAM OF DOING???

(Write down those dreams right here!)

VIII

Session Eight: Sensory Awareness

Every moment is a moment of learning. Life is the playground for our work...we experience through our senses. Charlotte Selver

As we age we may find our vision, hearing, taste, smell and other senses diminishing. The flow of neurotransmitters can be impaired. Temporal, occipital and parietal lobes may not be receiving as much information. This can correlate with memory loss and the possibility of acquiring age-related illnesses such as dementia and Alzheimer's.

Sensory awareness is a mindfulness practice to connect to ourselves and to cleanse and reconnect to, or reawaken, our authentic selves. It was originally developed in Europe by Elsa Gindler, and it was brought to the United States by one of her students, Charlotte Selver, in the 1930s.

With sensory awareness, we are not given lessons to be learned but an opportunity to begin the process of discovery. Sensory awareness gives us the gift to explore sensitively and to learn from that exploration. Through our senses we experience life. With sensing, we access greater inner quietness and clarity.

According to Gindler and Selver's work, sensory awareness helps us to restore our capacity to be more mindfully in the here and now and to awaken the possibilities within each one of us which may be dormant. Their philosophy says, "awakening means to follow faithfully what is needed."

Gindler and Selver also suggested that conscious living allows us to be in accord with our original nature. The more we do this, the more we discover.

Selver explained that sensory awareness is about presence-in-motion. She believed that mindful meditation is participation. In her sensory awareness training, she helped participants to experiment with all the simple activities of daily life; what we have done since birth and learned along the way, such as walking, standing, sitting, lying, moving, resting, speaking, listening, and seeing. She continued to explain that often we find ourselves full of fear, not wanting to allow changes.

Sensing emphasizes, refines, and enlarges us. "Sensing is getting more in touch with oneself, with others and with the world," taught Selver.

We attend to and respond to what is actually being sensed in the present moment. Being present is not necessarily thinking about something, it is more a matter of being aware of your immediate surroundings and of what is going on within you.

Selver wrote, "We have been thoroughly deprived of trusting the inner wisdom which each person has in him or herself. There lies a great unused richness in us, which we gradually have to dig out and develop. When you get to it, you will be astonished by what comes into the open which you didn't know was there."

In describing the study of sensing as simply a study of consciousness, Selver explains that when we are open to the reality of the moment, we are open to a meaningful connection with what we approach and what we do. We can practice sensory awareness during our everyday lives because we use our senses in everything we do. In sensory awareness, we are observers who are exploring perception without comparing, identifying, labeling, or attaching words.

In other words, we operate in a non-verbal world. Lee K. Lesser, one of Selver's students and now a sensory awareness teacher in the U.S., states that part of the work of sensory awareness is exploring what happens to us as adults. She poses these questions: How do we lose our innate responsiveness along life's journey and how can we rediscover and regain the natural ability and capacity we were born with and experienced as children?

We experience the world through our senses. Let us return to and reclaim our innateness, our childhood curiosity, and the observational skills that we had as children. Our brain will be reactivated and we will be reawakened.

Let's take the sensory walk!

Sensory Walk

Take a slow, sensory walk
Tune up the volume, let your lobes talk
Occipital, parietal, temporal, too
Let these parts work for you
Let your hearing be sharp
Your eyes brightly see
Your nose to smell, olfactory
Enhance memory, creativity
These are doors to authenticity
What do you see? What do you hear?
What smells are apparent to take you there?
Focus your attention
Be aware
The cortex will help you, be right there
Neurotransmitters flow
Connect and repair, your brain is rewiring
Elevate! Prepare!

IX

Session Nine: Nutrition, Physical Exercise and Healthy Lifestyle Choices

You are what you eat and the things you do,
change the firing patterns and chemical
composition of the brain.
Anthelme Brillat-Savarin

Now that you understand how the brain functions, there are several practical things you can do to enhance a holistic wellness program. Focusing on a healthy nutrition plan, regular physical exercise, and healthy lifestyle choices will assist you in transforming and maintaining your aging brain.

Nutrition and Healthy Lifestyle Choices

We are what we eat! We're sure you've heard this adage before. There is a new inverted pyramid which turns the former pyramid theory on its head. Grains and sugars are now the smaller, top part of the pyramid with fruits, protein, vegetables and healthy fats occupying the foundation or largest part of the pyramid. For more information on this new model, visit Dr. Joseph Mercola's website, www.mercola.com where he discusses his New Food Pyramid for Optimal Health.

In her March 2013 article in *Natural Awakenings* magazine titled "The Better Brain Diet: Eat Right to Stay Sharp," Lisa Marshall discussed the need for whole foods to include vegetables instead of white rice, pastas and sugary fruits. Citing studies published in the Journal of the American Medical Association and Archives of Neurology, she encourages us to eat more berries, kale, leafy greens and B vitamins. Marshall recommends curcumin, cinnamon, cloves, oregano, thyme, and rosemary to help dissolve plaque and improve memory.

Evidence points to the Mediterranean diet of olive oil, fish and vegetables as a healthy way to eat. Women who follow a Mediterranean diet in their 50s and 60s have 46% greater odds of surviving past age 70 with no chronic illness, physical impairments or memory problems, according to a large, new, Harvard study. The addition of "super foods" including fermented vegetables, whey protein, organic eggs, coconut oil, avocadoes, raw organic butter and pomegranates support a balanced metabolism. Linda and her husband have been eating a modified version of this diet for over thirty years and can attest to the fact that it helps support a holistic and healthy lifestyle.

David Zinczenko, in his book, *Eat This Not That*, recommends blueberries to promote long-term memory. He suggests coffee to boost short-term memory and attention.

Omega-3 fatty acids in the form of wild salmon and mackerel help prevent cognitive decline. Peppermint tea helps with concentration and performance of tedious tasks. Ingesting flax helps sharpen our senses. Flax is also widely accepted as a valuable natural supplement for digestion and regularity.

A recent article by Kim Erickson, in *Better Nutrition*, addresses the impact of one's lifestyle on the aging brain. It was the long-held belief, asserts Erickson, that brain aging and memory loss occurred because the neurons that we were born with were lost as we aged. Erickson explains that today's research affirms that this is *not* true. Dopamine controls the formation of new healthy neurons deep in the center of the adult brain. These new neurons move to the areas of the brain associated with higher brain functioning. Dopamine is the neurotransmitter, or chemical messenger, that forms in the brain when we learn new meaningful things and feel rewarded by experiences.

As we age we *do not* lose neurons. The normal aging process leaves most mental functions intact and may even allow the brain unique advantages that form the basis for what we call "wisdom."

According to data collected on 1,300 middle-aged people who took part in the *Framingham Offspring Cohort Study*, chronic health conditions such as diabetes and bad habits can contribute to cardiovascular disease that reduces blood flow to the brain. This causes the brain to utilize oxygen and protein less efficiently. Harmful habits can also increase inflammation and free-radical damage in the body.

Two recent studies published in the *Journal of Neurology*, reinforce evidence that heart health and brain health are linked. University of Pittsburgh researchers found that people with hardening of the arteries are more likely to have toxic plaque on their brains. Scientists in Berlin, Germany linked high blood sugar to memory problems.

Making healthy choices now will protect our brain from future harm. Sharpening our mental powers requires giving our brain what it needs to operate optimally. In the Kim Erickson article, she went on to mention a variety of herbs and supplements to help the brain fire on all cylinders. These included acytl-L carnitine, ginkgo biloba, bacopa, magnesium and citicoline.

In a recent article from the magazine *Better Nutrition*, a study from the annual report of the Cyclotron and Radioisotope Center at Tohoku University in Japan, cited that sniffing lavender created positive changes in heart rate and brain function among ten healthy young women. It further states that lavender has a pronounced positive effect on stress and anxiety. Other clinical trials suggest that its aroma can reduce intensity of pain and alleviate stress-related dysfunction. Lavender can help treat depression, respiratory ailments, fever, headache, skin problems and muscle pain as well as aiding more restful sleep.

During sleep the brain sweeps away wastes and toxins, a fact proven by scientists at The University of Rochester. Improving one's sleep reduces the risks of Alzheimer's and dementia. Reduction of stress and worry combined with exchanging old patterns for new positive thinking, helps to support improved quality of sleep.

Healthy fats support healthy minds. In fact, says Erickson, the brain is made of 60% fat. Good fatty acids are the building blocks of a properly functioning brain. A high quality fish oil is believed to be an essential component of a holistic and healthy diet. In the *American Journal of Clinical Nutrition*, research suggests that fish oil improves cognitive function and memory by suppressing inflammation and oxidative damage to the brain.

We now know that certain nutrients are essential for brain function and health. Dr. James Joseph at Tufts University discovered that *polyphenolic* compounds, found in many fruits and vegetables, can affect neuronal communication directly, so that neurons talk to each other more effectively. This can protect the aging brain from problems with nerve cell signals that are involved in memory and cognition.

A finding from research in the area of nutrition cites the benefits of cinnamon. Eating cinnamon significantly elevates the level of sodium benzoate in your brain. It also increases levels of chemicals referred to as *neurotrophic factors* in the brain. They stimulate the birth of new neurons and encourage survival of existing neurons, which is important to brain health, according to Gary Wenk at the Ohio State university.

An alarming statistic states that two thirds of Americans are overweight or obese. In truth, fats don't make us fat, processed sugar makes us fat. In our culture, our brains are thought to be as addicted to sugar as they would be on morphine or heroin. Sugar obesity is a major contributing factor to diabetes and other chronic diseases.

Dr. Robert Lustig, Professor of Pediatrics at the University of California, San Francisco, published an article in *Atlantic* magazine where he reported that most Americans eat twelve teaspoons of sugar a day or two tons of sugar in a lifetime. We must become more conscious and aware of what we put into our mouths! Our bodies are indeed our temples. We can begin to **XXX Change** and retrain our brains to seek and accept healthier, more nutritious ways of eating.

Lisa Turner, in *Better Nutrition*, discusses ways to rid the body of harmful substances. She suggests buying organic, grass-fed meats and poultry, avoiding eating food stored in cans, eliminating plastics for food storage, specifically any plastic item with the number seven on the container, buying organic nuts and cheese, eating from ceramic and stainless dishes, filtering water for drinking and showers, avoiding Styrofoam, and buying fragrance-free candles and air fresheners.

It's also beneficial to make popcorn from scratch, use natural beauty products, cook in stainless steel and cast iron rather than aluminum and become a restaurant vegan.

Healthy adjustments to one's lifestyle can also include humming and singing often, smiling and of course, laughing. We can eat more fresh foods, ditch packaged and fast foods, adopt a pet, be outdoors in sunlight, go barefoot, braless, and control the electronic pollution in our immediate environment. Take a warm bath with Epsom Salts. Turn off cell phones, computers and Wi-Fi at night. Intimacy and friendship are vital components of a healthy mind and lifestyle.

Our brain needs *metacognition* or the ability to be able to think about what we are thinking about. This need can be satisfied with daily written dialogue or journaling strengthening our senses and engaging in more meaningful pursuits. Our brain wants us to be more creative in everything we do from how we deal with our family to adding more time for music, dance, and art.

Our brain wants us to make the **XXX Change**: to be more grateful and to live with enhanced, elevated thoughts, feelings, moods, and realities. Our brain wants and needs more quiet time for meditation and prayer. Our brain wants more singing, dancing, and signing. All of these additions to our lifestyle will lower our stress and promote greater joy, vitality and longevity. We can tweak our brains to be more present, engaged, collaborative, intuitive, elevated, divine, focused, conscious, creative, authentic, playful, connected and excited about life!

Julia Boehm, Ph.D. and Laura Kubzansky, Ph.D., discovered that certain psychological traits such as optimism, positive emotions, and a sense of meaning offer measurable protection against heart attacks and strokes, slowing the process of aging and cardiovascular disease. The pair found that the most optimistic individuals had approximately 50% less chance of experiencing an initial cardiovascular event compared with less upbeat peers.

"The absence of the negative is not the same thing as the presence of the positive," notes Boehm. "Psychology has been trying to fix what's wrong with people, but there's also an increasing interest in what people might be doing right."

Dr. Deepak Chopra and Dr. Rudolph Tanzi in their book, *Super Brain: Unleashing the Explosive Power of Your Mind to Maximize Health, Happiness and Spiritual Well-Being*, invite us to ask ourselves, "How much time are we spending inside? What amount of our time do we spend on personal growth, appreciation, gratitude, intimacy, silence, meditation, contemplation, prayer, reflection, reading spiritual and inspirational poems, literature and stress management?"

Our entire Onto The Next team is becoming increasingly aware of the reality that living with an optimistic outlook is essential to holistic wellness. This mind-set requires a commitment of daily practice with intention, attention and constant repetition! Many studies have shown that a positive outlook can add up to seven years to one's life.

Water and Brain Energy

The brain is approximately 85% water. We need to drink one ounce of water for every three pounds of body weight. According to Dr. Corrine Allen, founder of the Advanced Learning and Development Institute, brain cells need two times more energy than other cells in the body. Water provides this energy more effectively than any other known substance. Dehydration causes the brain to shut down and not run at optimum efficiency.

Mental symptoms of dehydration include afternoon fatigue, difficulty focusing, increased stress, and headaches. Prolonged dehydration causes brain cells to shrink in size. This is most common in the elderly, many of whom tend to be chronically dehydrated for years.

Physical Exercise

Fresh air and physical exercise are essential for protection of the aging brain. According to Dr. Joseph Ratey, author of *Spark: The Revolutionary New Science of Exercise*, exercise promotes production of nerve-protecting compounds, increases blood flow to the brain, improves development and survival of neurons, promotes essential cell and tissue repair, and decreases the risk of heart and blood vessel disease.

In_*Train Your Mind, Change Your Brain*, Sharon Begley discusses the effect that exercise has on the increase of the number of stem cells that give rise to new neurons in the hippocampus. Remember that the hippocampus is directly related to memory!

She speaks of environmental enrichment that supports the survival of these cells. Enrichment affects the number of cells that survive and integrate into the circuitry.

Exercise releases endorphins and promotes brain health. Seriously! While many of us resist exercise, it has the best impact on us! After an appropriate workout, be it dancing, walking, riding a bicycle or swimming, you will actually "feel" great. It reduces stress and allows us to maintain emotional and mental balance.

Diana Nyad, the 64 year-old record-setting long distance swimmer that completed her swim from Havana, Cuba to Key West, Florida in August of 2013, spoke about some aspects of competitive edge that actually become *sharper* as we age.

She told reporters that she had more stamina, determination and confidence than when she was younger. Her first attempt to do the swim was thirty years earlier.

"...I'd like to prove to the other 60-year-olds that it is never too late to start your dreams," Nyad told those who asked about her motivation for the monumental task.

In an article in the AARP Bulletin, "Get Moving for a Healthy Brain," Margery Rosen discussed the latest research that proves cognitive decline is *not* inevitable. Since the brain continues to make new neurons and fine tune neural connections as long as we live, we can jumpstart that process with exercise.

John Medina, affiliate professor of bio-engineering at the University of Washington School of Medicine, says, "Aerobic exercise reduces the level of brain loss and keeps cognitive abilities sharp. It slashes the risk of Alzheimer's in half and the risk of dementia by 60%. Exercise spurs the release of 'Miracle-Gro' for the brain. Brain Derived Neurotrophic Factor (BDNF) stimulates formation of new neurons in the hippocampus, which is involved not only with memory but also the ability to plan, learn and make decisions. It also repairs cell damage and strengthens synapses."

A study done at the University of Illinois at Urbana-Champaign states, "People need to know that dementia is not inevitable!" They found that people 69-79 years old who had completed a six-month program of walking briskly on a regular basis, showed an increase in the size of the hippocampus and increased levels of BDNF comparable to those levels normally found in people almost two years younger.

A study in the *Archives of Internal Medicine* found that when women utilized weight training two times each week for six months, they had better focus and decision making skills than a control group who did only balance and toning exercises. They were also able to resolve conflicts much better.

"Benefits went beyond simply stemming memory loss. Subjects found actual improvements in their memory."

"Dance has recently become recognized as the greatest form of exercise", says Margery Rosen. She goes on to say, "Besides giving you a cardio boost, dance strengthens bones, works all the major muscle groups, builds stamina and improves balance, coordination and flexibility."

In Session Two, we shared that dancing is the best form of exercise as stated in the twenty-one year study at the Albert Einstein Institute in New York City.

Walking for forty minutes, three times a week can change your body as well as your brain. Standing intermittently, instead of sitting, has positive effects.

At www.mercola.com, Dr. Joseph Mercola's website, he says the best exercise is *anaerobic,* which is different from cardio or aerobic exercise. He suggests a weekly fitness routine of twenty minutes, three times each week. After a three-minute warm-up, using a recumbent bike, treadmill or stair climber, run or pedal as fast as you can for thirty seconds. Then walk or pedal at a normal speed for ninety seconds. Continue this sequence seven or eight times. Do this routine three times a week.

Add strength training for at least two days a week. In a week this doesn't add up to a great deal of time, yet the recommended hour is more effective than the equivalent of three to four one-hour aerobics classes a week.

"Spend less time and have a more effective workout," says Dr. Mercola. Linda has been following this regimen for several years and loves the results with the limited time she has to put in due to her busy schedule. She has more time for walking in the mountains or on the beach with her husband and dog who also benefit from her lifestyle.

Physical exercise produces new neurons and *dendrites* (tree-like extensions at the beginning of a neuron) to increase new neural pathways. Exercise can actually rewire and strengthen the brain.

According to the Cooper Institute in Dallas, which tracked nearly twenty-thousand physically fit adults over a twenty-four-year period, it is never too late to start exercising for brain health. Even if you have never exercised, it makes a difference, so, get started! What physical exercise do you follow each day?

Arthur Kramer and his team in their 2006 study, *Research on Cognition, Exercise, and the Aging Brain*, suggest that physical activity can have a neuroprotective effect on later-life cognition and our brains. It has been well established through many studies that exercise increases BDNF levels in the hippocampus to help protect the aging brain. In fact, some neurotransmitter systems are also positively affected by exercise.

Exercise boosts the blood flow to the brain spurring the release of BDNF. This chemical stimulates the formation of new neurons in the hippocampus, the area involved in memory. So, the more you exercise, the more you release BDNF into your brain. This is better for your memory and all of your mental processes.

Vigorous exercise can actually make you smarter and increase your creativity and memory. Even Cicero stated, "It is exercise alone that supports the spirit and keeps the mind in vigor."

X

Session Ten: Authenticity and Your "True North"

The privilege of a lifetime is to become who you truly are.
Carl Jung

Authenticity relates to our own inner power and what we feel in our heart. We are not talking about power over another person, but power that comes from being in an elevated place of positive feelings and mood. As our awareness of individual authenticity strengthens, we are able to **XXX Change** our fear, sadness, anger and doubt for elevated feelings of love, compassion, empathy, joy and trust. Through this evolution, we allow our brain to become a magnet for a more positive lifestyle.

We are learning to trust that whatever situation we find ourselves in, we can respond in ways that assure greater understanding and meaning in our lives. Every situation is an opportunity for positive change and greater consciousness. For a mind-expanding example, the Chinese symbol for *crisis* is the same as that for *opportunity*.

What Is Authenticity?

Our oneness
Our purpose
It sets us free
Our bliss, our soul, our unity
Our destiny
Our divinity
The love, joy, true reality
Our reason to be, our wisdom tree
The mountains, the sea
Seeds planted so deep
Our transparency
Faith to believe
Light to ignite, luminosity
Our source
Our flower
Empowered to be
Unleash, release
Authenticity, please!

Gary Zukov, in his book, *The Seat of the Soul,* speaks of the road to authentic power as being "what you feel through your heart." The way of the heart, notes Zukov, is one of compassion and emotional perception. When we begin to live authentically from an elevated space, we feel our emotions and learn to **XXX Change** the negative ones that no longer serve us. We begin to live at a higher frequency. We release patterns that are no longer necessary and can learn through wisdom instead of fear.

When we move toward authenticity, we become more focused and intentional in what we can accomplish. Zukov indicates that an authentically-empowered individual releases energy in love and trust. An authentic person is humble and inclusive of the beauty of each soul.

"Life," says Zukov, "is treasured and honored in all its forms." There is a collaboration and a connection of souls that begins to be revealed as one introduces ideas and concepts from an authentic place. There is no self-consciousness as one feels confident, humble and honored to be doing this work. An authentic being asks only for what it needs and is satisfied with the fulfillment of its *authentic* needs. There is an attitude of acceptance, joy, sharing, forgiveness, and respect.

"An authentic being," he says, "sees the perfection of each situation and every aspect serves as a beautiful learning that everything is designed for wholeness and perfection."

As we walk on this earth, accumulating years and wisdom, we come to realize that we are all here having signed a contract or agreement to fulfill our life's purpose. This contract holds the clues to our authentic being. We have been moving toward this authenticity since our birth, with the amassing of experiences leading us to who we are and what we are here to do at this very moment. This is our wisdom.

What are the experiences that we have that allow us to lose sense of time and space? What are the things that bring us great joy? What do we do that allows us to feel deep satisfaction from inside? What are our gifts? What are our talents? What is our bliss? This is our authentic self beckoning, the part of us that we call our *soul*. The planet needs this!

As we live more authentically, we begin to find a greater trust in the road we have been traveling and the part we are being asked to play. As our trust grows, we lose more and more of the obstacle-thinking that keeps us from moving forward. There is a sense of excitement, connection and joy as we learn to use our intuition, collaborate and trust in this way. There is a feeling of peace and satisfaction that what is happening is part of a much greater plan.

Other people are drawn to this experience and become part of the process adding their own authenticity. Like magnets, positive energy attracts. What we put out is often how we are perceived and what we receive.

With authenticity and trust comes gratitude for all that we have received and are here to participate in. We are grateful for each breath we take and the time and space to do all we have been sent here to do. Our "True North" evolves from our trust in the direction that we are going. Continuously checking in with our honest feelings, we are shown the way to evolve.

We grow from our heart, feeling deeper love and compassion for all human beings. We realize we cannot judge another person or give advice. Each soul is on his or her own journey. When we trust and respect that, we can live together in a supportive, non-competitive world.

Like a beautiful old piece of furniture hidden beneath layers of paint, our authentic self is buried beneath layers and layers of conditioning. Over the years, external influences in our lives such as certain people, "shoulds," "should nots," our past experiences, and old messages have muted our authentic self. We must uncover, dig deep, and discover who we are designed to be. This elevates us to joy, peace, and a positive state of being.

Authenticity is a process. Ask yourself questions repeatedly and intentionally. As we question, we peel away the layers and uncover what is hidden beneath. It's like finding a "pearl of great value."

Look Inside

Look inside, you will find
This is where the answers lie.
Nothing outside will provide
The riches that reside inside.
It's time for humanity to comply
It's not about what's acquired outside.
A bigger residence or faster ride
Will not abide—instead we must find...
Our value, vision, voice to acquire:
It's time to comply and rewire.
All here to fulfill this desire—
The divine design will inspire,
Purpose, passion, inner fire.
So look within, each one to find
The authentic self residing inside!

In his book, *True North*, Harvard Professor Bill George asks, "Why would you think someone else knows you better than you know yourself?"

He suggests that we start to listen to our own inner voice and act accordingly. George believes that people, with no map to follow, get lost in their own lives and they don't know how to follow their internal compass. In other words, they don't know which way is "True North."

In his book, George poses an important question for us to ponder. "What are the most important things you want to do?"

When we can answer this question, then we can plan. We'll know in which direction we should be headed. This knowledge about ourselves will help us to find clarity and direction—and our "True North"!

True North

To find your True North
Is the new order
Moving forth
Through fire, wind, water
Forward motion
Divine devotion
It's now in your court
The star of last resort
Don't lose the motion!

XI

Session Eleven: Gratitude, Joy, and Wisdom

Be present in all things and thankful for all things. Maya Angelou

Joy comes from within, more permanent. Happiness is out there and can be taken away at any moment. Hank

Wisdom begins in wonder. Socrates

Marianne Williamson, in her book, *The Age of Miracles*, speaks of many who have been split off from their authentic selves and their souls. We spend a lifetime wandering in an outer world which is not our real home.

Our inner world is who we truly are. As we age we come to appreciate that, and can begin to return to our true feelings of authenticity and love.

Williamson discusses that as our bodies begin to slow down, we can do *more*, not less. We can take more time to re-awaken our senses, feel our feelings and **XXX Change** old tape loops, transforming our brain and mind to be in an elevated, energized and creative place.

Gratitude and Joy

Sit down in a beautiful place—
Take a deep breath and look at the space.
Feel a happy memory you can trace
Or a near-happy memory to bring a smile to
your face.
Recall it now in this beautiful space.
Were you with someone, what did you do?
To bring this happiness back to you.
Feel this joy you can now review.
What makes you feel grateful deep inside?
Friends, family, opportunities that arrive?
What is it that keeps your joy alive?
Feel this now from deep inside.
Think of all you are thankful for...
People, places, that which you adore!
Bring this back in your mind to explore.

We become more deeply in touch with our *knowing* from within. We might think of this as *intuition.* Using our senses, our feelings and our intuition, we come to realize it is time to live from a deeper place. We discover our wisdom, which comes from understanding our value and the many experiences that have made us who we are today.

This wisdom brings us closer to our personal inner truths. We no longer need to fit into someone else's picture of pretty or successful or rich. Our uniqueness of self is beckoning to be acknowledged, nurtured, loved, and given a voice. We can accept ourselves with all our wrinkles, bulges, curves, missteps, faults and oddities. This is what makes us real and human.

Everyone makes mistakes and has regrets. This is the nature of the human condition. Still, it's time to let go of the past. This is the opportunity to be more authentic. Just like the story "The Velveteen Rabbit" we *can* become real and feel loved.

We can speak our truth and fall in love with ourselves, feeling an inner joy and self-acceptance. As we move toward our wholeness, we can celebrate, feel peaceful and be free. Dr. Christine Northrop, MD, notes that when passing a mirror, we should gaze into our own eyes and say, "I love you."

As we embrace our aging, we become aware that we are not the center of the universe. We are part of a grander design, a divine plan. Our spirituality awakens and blossoms. Dr. George Vaillant, MD, suggests that our maturity allows us to develop a more nuanced emotional life and deeper spiritual appreciation. This is the core as we acknowledge our wisdom. As negative labels are **XXX Changed** and our brain becomes rewired, we are able to sustain elevated moods. After a time, this becomes our new personality. We are fulfilling our potential.

When we begin to identify with our spiritual existence, says Marianne Williamson, our attitude becomes one of deep appreciation and gratitude. We take the time to feel this gratitude as we exercise more regularly in the morning, pay attention to the food we are ingesting and acknowledge people in our family as well as our friends. Understanding that an attitude of gratitude, joy, and love has a higher frequency than a negative attitude does, we will attract more like-minded people and opportunities to ourselves when we operate from that positive place. This elevated awareness will fuel new thoughts and creations. Gratitude is a sacred practice. The intentional act of moving toward gratitude helps to physically shift the neuro-chemical landscape of our brain.

We all have challenges. How we respond to difficult moments will dictate their impact on us and determine our ability to accept our circumstances and see opportunities. As long as we are alive, we can learn and move to a place of greater understanding, consciousness, and ultimately enlightenment.

In other words, as the anonymous quote says, "It is not happy people who are thankful, it is thankful people who are happy." A number of medical research studies have documented that patients with critical, even terminal illnesses, fare far better with a positive, powerful outlook on life than those who do not.

Ram Dass (Dr. Richard Alpert, Harvard), states in his latest book, *Polishing The Mirror,* "He who has so little knowledge of human nature as to seek happiness by changing anything but his own disposition, will waste his life in fruitless efforts." He further states, "Just keep working on yourself so you are radiating love for each of the beings in your life."

Rick Hanson, in his DVD, *Being for Yourself,* helps us to understand that being our own best friend has a warm, compassionate, caring component that allows the hormones *oxytocin* and *estrogen* to flow. In other words, when we emotionally love and embrace our authentic selves, our bodies support that and make us feel good, too!

When we begin to treat our lives as if they matter, we *want* to assist and befriend others. Joy is our birthright. Mary Oliver, the poet, states, "This is your one wild and precious life."

George Vaillant, in *Spiritual Evolution*, tells us that the human brain is hardwired for loving, spiritual resilience, and community welfare. We are meant to care about ourselves and those around us. Besides cultural and genetic evolution, adult development supports human spirituality. Vaillant goes on to say that positive emotions grow as we mature. Our frontal lobes become wired to the limbic system. Planning is linked with passion. Being positive and elevated is critical to preserving our memory, as the hippocampus, which is responsible for memory, responds to positive emotions.

As elders, we now have the opportunity to use *both* sides of our brain and unite cognition with musicality and intuition. The ***Multi-Modal Method (MMM),*** described in Session Two, pp 21-34, is designed to support this critical integration.

We are in our golden years, the time to elevate love, unity, community, and being one with the universe. We are moving toward mystical oneness, according to George Vaillant. The Dalai Lama says, "We are all one."

With our wisdom and feelings of love, we can begin to trust and have faith that the world has meaning and so does our role in it. We can practice loving-kindness and trust in that which we cannot see, but know exists. We begin to value our inner world and move toward illumination, awe and the understanding of what is sacred.

In *Spiritual Evolution*, Vaillant discusses the limbic system, deep in the mammalian brain, as being the seat of mystical experience, and where the emotions of love, joy, empathy, forgiveness, and compassion live. As it links with the frontal cortex which is responsible for planning, we can begin to envision a future where we are connected in relationships, forgiveness, healing and unconditional love.

The tiny sovereign nation of Bhutan operates based on a historically relevant Gross Domestic Happiness value system. The country has focused on growing both materially and spiritually. *Citizen well-being takes precedence over economic growth.* The reigning definition of happiness involves peace, contentment and living in harmony with all creation.

Martin E. Seligman, the author of *Flourish: A Visionary New Understanding of Happiness and Well-Being*, discusses how writing down three blessings every day, being an active listener, and being present in a relationship can strengthen human bonds and make us happy. He further notes, increasing meaning in our lives by including more "we" than "I" can make us feel good.

Ideas from www.AuthenticHappiness.com, suggest that we identify our strengths and use more of them. Whatever you love to do needs to be acknowledged and given the time and space to do it. Reach out to others. Helping those in need fulfills us and allows us to feel the joy from inside.

Wisdom, according to the Dalai Lama, is an ongoing process and is not static. It's not a divine gift limited to a select few. The Dalai Lama continually says, "Keep working on it."

Wisdom involves an integration of knowledge, experience, and deep self-awareness that incorporates tolerance for the uncertainties of life. It supports balance, awareness and the ability to see the big picture while maintaining a sense of peace.

We find the Peace Prayer of St. Francis de Assisi very helpful in our daily lives, especially in times when our own peace is being interrupted by life's circumstances!

The Peace Prayer of St. Francis de Assisi

Lord, make me an instrument of your peace.
Where there is hatred let me sow love.
Where there is injury let me sow forgiveness.
Where there is doubt let me sow faith.
Where there is despair, let me give hope.
Where there is sadness, let me give joy.
O Master, grant that I may not so much seek
compassion, but to give compassion.

To our attentive readers, this prayer is a beautiful example that articulates the *XXX Change*!

XII

Session Twelve:
Creativity and Memory

*Creativity is about giving the world something
it didn't know it was missing.*
Daniel Pink

*The authentic self is the best part of a human
being. When your authentic self awakens and
becomes stronger than your ego, then you will
make a difference in this world. You will enter
into a partnership with the creative.*
Andrew Cohen

Creativity

"Creativity is who we are," says theologian Matthew Fox, in his book, *Creativity*. It is a complex, cognitive process, and combines elements of emotion, planning, and sensory perception.

It can also redeem us and save our species. The international award-winning post-traumatic specialist Dr. Clarissa Pinkola Estes has written that *all* men and women are born gifted.

We believe, as elders, we are here to uncover or re-discover our gifts and talents. Given the state of the world right now, we must begin to look inside, utilize a greater portion of our brain, use our creative imagination, and be awakened to new ideas and resources in order to save our planet.

Fox speaks about creative courage as the discovery of new forms, new symbols, and new patterns on which society can be built. As previously discussed, presently the left-brain mind has been the dominant force on the planet.

Creativity has been diminished in importance in families, education, government, and business. We *must* get back to the creative part of ourselves and give birth to that. Austrian psychoanalyst and teacher Otto Rank said that creativity is central to our hearts and souls as human beings. It is on the same level as love and is a sign of our health and well-being.

"When we begin to dialogue with our own heart, we will become the artist we are," says Fox.

When we allow ourselves to engage in music, dance, drumming, and the arts—the activities of our ancestors and the indigenous people—we celebrate life. Marvelous things begin to happen. We are engaging with the source, the divine, and our authentic selves.

A return to our origins, asserts Fox, is long overdue. When we engage in the tools of the *Multi-Modal Method (MMM)* we reflect the innate, preverbal knowledge that has evolved from our ancestors. These modalities are the foundation of language and literacy. They are the core elements of our creative being. We aren't the only ones who think this way. In Fox's book *Creativity*, he shares the following observations:

♥ The *Kabbalah* teaches that the fierce power of the imagination is a gift from God

♥ Thomas Aquinas (philosopher and theologian) believed that the human mind is infinite and imagination contains all things.

♥ In the Celtic belief, the soul is the place where imagination lives.

♥ Meister Ekhart believes that creativity causes the soul to rejoice.

- Hildegaard of Bingen believed the spirit's work and the artist's work is to awaken all things. She felt the truth of the deep down holiness of all things ought to be enough to awaken us from our slumber.
- Author Anais Nin said that to write, sing and dance is to *taste life twice.*

Creativity takes us back to our preverbal, pre-rational selves. We experience freedom!

Matthew Fox believes that when you bring forth that which is within you, it will save you. According to Fox, creativity is "...where the divine and human meet."

Creativity happens at the border between chaos and order. In other words, chaos is a prelude to creativity. As children, we were all artists. As we age, we are continually being called upon to be artists in our own unique way. What has happened with our creativity since our childhood? What ignites our creativity now?

In reference to discovering our creative selves in the here and now, Fox continues to ask us, "What are we waiting for?" He challenges us to remove any obstacles, let go and get moving. For, as Fox proclaims, "creativity is a choice."

There is a new study underway to examine the power of art to stave off dementia. At the St. Michael's Hospital Memory Clinic, in Toronto, Canada, they are looking at the role of creativity as it relates to dementia and Alzheimer's. They are finding that a subject's personality transforms when given a sketch pad, piano or music for listening. The doctors at St. Michael's found that their participants have developed unique neural networks that are more resistant to the effects of diseases like Alzheimer's, dementia, vascular dementia and strokes.

"The neural networks of creativity might be stronger than the pathologies. The common denominator is the art...any kind of art." Patients with Parkinson's disease who studied dance required less medication. The reason? Music and rhythm are the boosters. Art not only expands our minds, but physically bolsters them against disease.

When Linda took a hiatus from the clinical and traditional world of speech pathology, she embarked on a quest to pursue a deeper awareness of how creativity affects learning and artistic expression.

Linda created the **Multi-Modal Method (MMM)** as an evolution of her own creative exploration. She implemented the tools of music, sign language, dance, meditation and visualization to support early language and literacy success. This was an innovative and effective methodology, combining the use of preverbal tools to enhance early language and literacy development. Through many subsequent years of applying these modalities, she came to understand the critical importance that creative pathways play in learning for all children as well as aging adults.

It is time to remove the obstacles to our creativity. Bid farewell to fears, doubts, guilt, and lack of faith and trust. They do not allow us to be who we truly are. We are wisdom, we are compassion, we are joy and delight!

All of this is experienced when we begin to be our creatively authentic selves. We become more interested in life, community and sharing. We experience renewed vitality and feelings of being valued, appreciated and loved. There is a profound connection with our divinity.

Matthew Fox invites us to call on our angels and our guides to move us in the direction we need to go. When we begin to do this, we become open to meeting the right people who will share our journey. We will be shown the books we need to read, places we need to be and numerous opportunities will come our way. We will be living in synchronicity.

Meditation helps us to accept, relax and focus. It allows our mind to become less overwhelmed and crowded so that we can be mindfully guided on this new journey. We are able to praise all that is in nature and honor the divinity within. Feeling more openness and joy, we let go and explore greater possibilities for our lives.

With joy, we are engaged in the work we were sent here to do. There may be dark moments in our lives, feelings of fear, sadness, and anger, but we can move through them, exchanging the negative for more positive ways of being.

In the visualization experience during our seminar, "Transforming Your Aging Brain," we are guided to see ourselves doing what we are meant to do. The experiences that bring us elevated feelings of love, compassion, empathy, and joy are supportive of our authentic, creative selves. All humans suffer and this cannot be denied, yet we can learn from our suffering. Creativity makes use of the suffering as well as the joy.

When we are in the flow of our creative selves, much of our brain is engaged. The parietal, temporal, and occipital lobes are activated. We are motivated from the inside to improvise. Instead of being self-conscious we operate from a non-judgmental place of possibility.

Shelly Carson, in her book, *Your Creative Brain*, speaks of the receptive brain of creative people being open to a state of trance: able to go into *alpha* and *theta* states. If you have ever heard the term, "being in the zone," you will understand this concept. That place is mindful and non-judgmental. Carson says to speak to the back of your brain and ask it for novel ideas.

We can turn down the volume from the amygdala and be open to the feelings of the limbic area. The prefrontal cortex can be asked to be quiet as the back of the brain is called into action.

"We all have creative brains," says Carson. Through conscious effort we can turn the volume up and down and master activation of circuits that call for new and exciting ideas. This can become a conscious process and an important asset in negotiating this changing and challenging world. Carson believes it's time to make a contribution—to discover, innovate and produce as a part of the 21st Century's Golden Age.

Dr. Gene Cohen in his 2002 study, *The Creative Age: Awakening the Human Potential in the Second Half of Life,* described three aspects of creativity among older adults:

1. Creativity strengthens our morale later in life. We feel better when we view problems with new perspectives and creativity.

2. Creativity is our greatest legacy. We are invaluable role models for future generations and can shape thinking and social policies on aging.

3. Creativity contributes to our physical health as we age. Creativity promotes well being and an optimistic view on aging.

Cohen further believed that creativity is connected to positive brain health. "Brains create new brain cells as long as we are encouraged to keep trying new pursuits." He also said, "When we enter the middle years of life, both sides of the brain are not only used but they work more closely together."

Susan Krauss Whitbourne, a professor at the University of Massachusetts-Amherst, believes that the aging process is kinder to the creative, active and flexible mind. She believes that friendships are one way to keep your brain in top form, as is having a flexible mental attitude. Whitbourne cited Schaie and Willis' study that discovered that a flexible mental attitude staves off intellectual declines among people well into their seventies and eighties.

Whitbourne suggests that memory, attention, and the ability to shift mental focus are all necessary operations for creativity. Openness to new ideas and a flexible attitude toward change are the essence of creativity. Creative endeavors are just plain good for helping to slow the decline of our mental capabilities.

The aging brain is quite resilient, and can be stimulated to innovate, create and contribute in remarkable ways. Unfortunately, a decline in creativity can result from elders not being challenged. So, nudge your neurons, shake things up, stay physically active, and seek out new environments that support your insights and creativity!

Creativity and memory go hand in hand and cannot exist without each other! Have fun with this next poem!

Creativity, It's Time

Picasso once said:
"The enemy of creativity is good sense."
Think about intelligence—
It's not creative
When it makes good sense.
Creativity is making new brain connections
Going off in different directions.
Combining science with the soul—
New awareness—
Letting go of control.
Here's to Picasso and the creative mind
Let's celebrate this for humankind.
It's our evolution, I remind,
With joy and love we will find
Creativity—It's time!

Creativity and Play

"Almost all creativity involves purposeful play," said Abraham Maslow. And behavioral psychologist Linda Naiman notes, "When we engage in what we are naturally suited to do, our work takes on the quality of play and it is play that stimulates creativity."

It has been said that play makes you smarter, more creative, and happier by spurring the growth of neurons and making new connections in our brain. Play arouses curiosity, strengthens our connections to others, stimulates our imagination, triggers endorphins to lift us and elevates us to a more joyful place.

As you read this section (and after) take a moment and think back to your childhood. What are your play histories? What brought you pure joy? Where were your play spaces? Did you have a special place where you could think and imagine? What were your play tools?

As we think about these questions, visualize what could be a catalyst to jumpstart what is next. Open your mind, let it run free. Imagine! Play!

"Play is more than just fun," according to Dr. Stuart Brown, a pioneer in research on play. Play lights up the brain in the areas of clarity and memory. Dr. Brown has studied the power of play for many years. He calls play a "state of being, purposeless, fun and pleasurable."

Play is a catalyst. Give yourself permission to play and surround yourself with playful people, and of course, children.

Play is often absent as we age, so we have to set an intention to invite it back into our lives. Somewhere between our childhood and adulthood, many of us stop playing, exchanging play for serious pursuits. Here are three questions to consider:

1. Have you retained your spirit of play in your adulthood?
2. Do you value play, but have difficulty doing it often?
3. Have you left play behind you, leaving it only as a memory from your childhood?

Laura Seargeant Richardson, in a keynote speech at MIT's Sandbox Summit, suggested, "Play is the greatest natural resource in a creative economy." She believes that in the future, economies will be driven by what she calls "play capital" rather than by financial or scientific capital.

Richardson suggests that innovation in our country will involve highly advanced forms of play. She calls this form of play *superpowers*—natural abilities and skills that we intentionally foster—helps us adapt and thrive in a complex global environment.

Play brings us joy and happiness. It is vital for creativity and healthy relationships. It is simultaneously relaxing and stimulating for our brain and body. Play is a necessity because it makes us feel alive and connected.

Remember, R.C. Ferguson once said, "People are getting old when they walk around a puddle instead of through it!"

When was the last time you walked, jumped, or splashed in a puddle? So, what are you waiting for?

Memory

Memory has been defined as a process of information retention in which our experiences are archived and then recovered when we recall them. Edward Forster defined it this way: "Memory is the cabinet of imagination, the treasury of reason, the registry of conscience and council chamber of thought."

Memories are enhanced patterns of neuronal interconnections which are subject to continual change. Think of looking into a kaleidoscope. The shapes, colors and lengths of color all change with even the slightest movement. Those neuronal pathways and connections are like that!

Memory is divided into *long-term* and *short-term* memory. Short-term memory, also called *working* memory, is the brain's system for remembering information that's "in use." Most people can only hold five to ten items in their short-term memory at one time. Long-term memory is that part of our memory storage system that has unlimited capacity to retain information over an extended period of time.

There are three types of long-term memory:

- Procedural memory is for motor or skill learning
- Declarative memory is for facts

- Remote memory is for memories acquired early in life

Both short-term and long-term memory are composed of three processes: *encoding or acquisition, storage,* and *retrieval.*

Creating a memory begins with encoding or acquisition. It is rooted in the senses and begins with perception. Each sense travels to the hippocampus. It is then stored using the language of electricity and chemicals. Nerve cells connect with other nerve cells called synapses. The electrical firing triggers the release of chemical messengers called neurotransmitters.

With each new experience, the brain slightly rewires the physical structure and *neuroplasticity* happens. When we want to retrieve a memory that exists on an unconscious level, we can bring it into our conscious mind at will.

Memory and creativity go hand in hand. Short-term memory is stored in the temporal lobe and sent to long-term memory in the frontal cortex, our "hard drive."

The part of your brain essential for making new memories is the hippocampus. Creativity is supported in the temporal, parietal, and occipital lobes as well through sensory input. When we are thinking of novel ideas, new pathways are created and neurotransmitters flow.

This is the experience created for participants at our **Onto the Next** seminars. Throughout the seminar, new meaningful concepts are combined with interactive exercises that allow the brain to feel rewarded. Neurotransmitters flow and fire new neurology in the brain. This is how we transform our aging brain! Visit **www.ontothenext.org**

By being creative, we can protect our memory and minimize the risks of dementia, Alzheimer's, stroke, and Parkinson's disease. Our memories are a reflection of an entire lifetime.

A highly recognized Canadian neurosurgeon, Wilder Penfield, discovered something fascinating about memory. While probing the temporal lobes of patients with epileptic seizures he touched and stimulated the temporal lobes of the brain. The patients remembered previous experiences vividly.

"They were electrical activations of the sequential record of consciousness that had been laid down during the patients' earlier experiences. The brain stores everything its owner has ever experienced in its original form."

Everything we've ever experienced is there in the subconscious. The question is how do we retrieve it. *Focused intent* is the key to memory retrieval.

It was previously thought that aging causes loss of brain cells and that the hippocampus could lose five percent of its nerve cells with each passing decade. If that was true, by the time we have reached our eighties, we might have a total loss of forty percent.

It was also believed that aging led to a drop in the production of a neurotransmitter called *acetylcholine*. Acetylcholine is the primary brain chemical communicator for thought, learning, and memory. However, in the last five years, some very promising research by Dr. Michela Gallagher of Johns Hopkins gives a new insight into aging and the brain. She believes that old brain cells don't die, they just malfunction. So, if that hypothesis is true, and research is certainly pointing in that direction, what can we do to promote positive brain health and overall wellness for our aging body, mind, soul and spirit?

We can use the ***Multi-Modal Method (MMM)*** and practice intention, attention, and daily repetition with these tools.

We must stay conscious of our attitude if we are to stay healthier in every aspect. A positive, energetic and generous state of mind seems to be the deciding factor in some studies of the aging brain. Beatrice Seagull, author of *Mind Your Mind*, suggests that studies also show that prolonged stress kills off cells in the hippocampus that affect memory and retrieval.

There is a form of Alzheimer's known as *asymptomatic*, which means that even though the pathology confirmed the presence of

Alzheimer's in a person after they passed on, they exhibited *none* of the symptoms in their daily life. Researchers are confident in saying today that staying physically active, being generous and involved with others, and keeping our minds active with the arts or studies allows our brains to rewire and therefore stave off the debilitating effects of Alzheimer's and other dementias. The majority of people who had no symptoms were found to be those with elevated attitudes and positive outlooks on life.

Memory is supported by creativity. When we are interested and motivated to learn, it is easier to remember. It is important to make connections and see the patterns in anything new that we learn. Creating pictures or stories in our imagination of what we want to learn allows us to create and retain the memory. Interpersonal relationships also support memory.

Interesting new research by Dr. Joseph Mercola (www.mercola.com) explains that the simple body movement of clenching your fist may change the way your brain functions by boosting your memory significantly.

In these ways, we are engaging more of the brain to help us remember. Jonathan Hancock and Cheryl Buggy, in their book, *Successful Memory Techniques*, discuss the importance of place to help us remember. When we walk into a room and cannot remember what we came to do, if we return to the place where we thought of what we needed to retrieve, we can often remember what we were looking for.

Songs, tunes, or poems help us to remember. Both sides of the brain are being engaged which makes remembering much easier. There is an area on the right side of the brain that corresponds directly to the language area on the left side. The melody and rhythm of music supports the language area. Stories are another tool to assist us in remembering. Imagination allows us to make something memorable.

Saint Augustine said, "People travel to wonder at the highest of mountains, at the vast compass of the ocean, at the circular motion of the stars, and they pass by themselves without wondering." Within us is an incredible universe to explore, and with our imaginations, we can create anything.

Dr. Bruno Furst, in his book, *Conscious Remembering*, tells us to concentrate, listen, observe and remember. He also mentions using our senses and creativity to improve our memory. Making associations and connecting new ideas to old familiar ones, will assist memory.

The prefrontal cortex or executive center helps us to stay vigilant, observe, concentrate and focus. Our imagination, elevated emotions, low stress and a positive attitude all support healthy memory. We must consciously commit things to memory. Visualization allows us to form a mental image to assist us. When we cannot remember something, if we relax and actually state, "I'll think of it," we are putting the possibility into our brain of coming up with the answer.

Linda uses this phrase and at the same time, visualizes a small counter-clockwise circle on the back right side of her brain. Forgotten material is often retrieved. She also finds signing a person's name by using the manual sign alphabet (finger spelling), allows her to remember and retrieve the name. Deepak Chopra has stated that clenching the right fist helps put things into memory. Clenching the left fist helps us retrieve information.

A recent article in the AARP bulletin from June/July 2013, speaks of boredom being the enemy of memory, and creativity being the rejuvenator. Breaking old habits opens up millions of neurological synapses. Brain health is tied to physical health and novelty. Volunteer, take a class, tutor, meet with friends, take a new route, even get out of bed on the opposite side, or brush your teeth with the non-dominant hand.

In *Train Your Mind, Change Your Brain*, Sharon Begley recommends physical exercise to increase new neurons in the hippocampus. Participation in activities that enrich our daily lives supports the number of cells that survive and integrate into the circuitry. Begley believes that age-related decline comes from weaker and less accurate sensory input.

We can protect our brains by taking a proactive, conscious stance to support our creative, physical, cognitive, social, and spiritual development well into our later years. By using the tools available in this text and by practicing the **Multi-Modal Method (MMM)** we can rewire our aging brains to be more aware of our senses and be positive and passionate about life.

It is essential that we reduce stress. We can remain positive and maintain emotional and mental equanimity through the use of meditation, prayer, healthy foods and regular exercise. These simple practices can help us live longer, healthier and with a better quality of life!

Each of these preverbal, pre-rational modalities, individually and together, support a strong memory. In combination, they enhance memory exponentially and can help minimize the risks of dementia and Alzheimer's.

DOODLING ENCOURAGED

XIII

Session Thirteen: A Call to Action and Leaving a Legacy

You must live in the present, launch yourself on every wave, find your eternity in each moment. Fools stand on their island of opportunities and look toward another land. There is no other land, there is no other life but this.
Henry David Thoreau

Man's main concern is not to gain pleasure or to avoid pain but rather to see a meaning in his life.
Viktor Frankl

A Call to Action

This is a call to action
A universal shift—
Divine intervention,
The brain taking on new patterns.
To be in the moment is what matters,
"Let go of the old," is the adage.
Find your new life,
Your purpose, your passion!
Seeds planted before you were born—
Now to be harvested with each new dawn.
How can we help others fulfill
Their dreams, their longings
The divine will?
Deep from within, we can begin
To live an authentic life with vision.
This is a call to action,
Let the celebration begin!

In his book, *Living with Purpose*, Ken Dychtwald poses what is a challenge to those of us who are part of this new Golden Age.

We have the opportunity to rewire our brain as we **XXX Exchange** old messages and feelings: fear becoming faith, anger becoming joy, and pain becoming love. By uncovering our dreams and gifts, we establish a conduit for sharing and giving.

Joseph Campbell states, "Follow your bliss and doors will open where there were no doors before." We can reject the idea that we have climbed the mountain, reached the pinnacle, and now it's time to retire to a rocking chair or a Lazy Boy where we'll become useless and forgotten.

It's time to create a new vision for our lives based upon what fuels our passion. We can make a difference in ways we cannot begin to imagine. Dychtwald discusses doing something significant, something that gives meaning and satisfaction. This is called *leaving a legacy*. He speaks of "finding a new purpose, to give life meaning that might become our most joyous and nourishing time on earth."

As the generation of Baby Boomers who have shaped society and history repeatedly, it is our time to bring our wisdom to the world. What are we here to do that will make the world a better place? We must self-actualize and engage in our global community. Our vision, value and vitality will empower a deeper sense of trust and hope for future generations and the planet. Mining our talents will give us more energy. Wisdom produces appreciation and creativity.

Using our creativity will give us a greater sense of our authentic selves. This is a component of the "sharing continuum" and strengthens our legacy. As we age we are keenly aware of the concept that we should live our lives as if each day is our last. This brings a deeper meaning to each day. None of us know what the future holds. Let's uncover our dreams and pursue them with intention, focus and conviction.

As we discover our individual potential, we invoke the laws of *synchronicity*. We attract events, opportunities and the people who support us on our journey. This is a time for new friendships that will propel us to do greater, more exciting things. These relationships become a part of our new support network. We are all evolving toward self-realization. Winston Churchill noted, "United we stand, divided we fall." By working collaboratively, we can accomplish much more than we could ever have accomplished individually.

Mirror neurons were first discovered in the early 1980s through the 1990s by Dr. Giacomo Rizzolatti and a team of Italian neuroscientists and researchers at the University of Parma, Italy. They are types of brain cells that fire and respond quickly when we either perform an action or witness someone else perform the same action. In other words, neurons "mirror" the behavior of others.

Mirror neurons could explain how and why we "read" other people's minds and empathize with others. It gives us the ability to instinctively and immediately understand what other people are experiencing. For example, if someone is struggling with an emotionally challenging issue, in essence, we "feel" their pain or discomfort. Mirror neurons are helping neuroscientists reinterpret the neurological underpinning of social interactions, and the understanding of goals and intentions.

According to Marco Iacoboni at UCLA, "these neurons are important for understanding intentions as well as actions." Dr. Vittorio Gallese, a colleague of Rizzolatti's concurs and states, "We don't have to think about what other people are doing or feeling, we simply know."

We have the neurological ability to reinvent ourselves. As we build meaning into our visions, the brain sees this as a "call to action." Energy flows where attention goes. The synaptic connections energized by our habitual attention eventually become more or less chemically hard-wired into our neural network. This process is called *Hebbian learning* after Donald Hebb, a Canadian psychologist, who expressed the theory of neurological adaptation.

We are hard-wired to care about what we leave behind when we are gone. Our legacy is what we create during a lifetime to benefit future generations: that which is left behind without expecting anything in return.

Angela Maiers, the owner of *Choose2Matter*, states that there are seven key points for us to know in understanding that we matter. "The seven points are: you are enough, you have influence, you are a genius, you have a contribution to make, you have a gift that others need, you are the change and your action defines your impact."

Ken Dychtwald discovered the "four pillars of legacy." These elements are:

- ♥ values and life lessons
- ♥ instructions and wishes to be fulfilled
- ♥ possessions of emotional value
- ♥ property and money

In a recent survey conducted by Dychtwald, most people reported values and life lessons as the most important components of one's legacy.

In our role as elders, it is important to think about those to whom we are passing the legacy. We need to keep planting seeds even though we may never see the fruit. Although this may be challenging, we need to enjoy the planting. This challenge is accomplished in the cortex, the part of the brain that likes to plan and organize. Our true mark and legacy will emerge from the creativity we have applied to real challenges in our lives. Our legacy is the fruit of living authentically, molded by specific life experiences.

Promoting our legacy triggers happy chemicals in the brain! As Erik Erikson said, "I am what survives of me."

Creating our legacy is an intentional process throughout our lives. What will we leave as a legacy to our family, community, and the world at large?

Read "Road to Forever" and "The Elder Seal" on the next two pages.

Road to Forever

The journey of life never ends
As the road shifts and turns
Over the mountains, around the bends,
We are given all of life's lessons.
Though we must with our eyes remain on high
We can visualize the place—we arrive.
It is what we learn as we take the ride
That makes it worthy of the prize.
The soul contains a map of the way
And with each breath we move through the day.
Our passions, longings and events all play
A part in the art that our life displays.
Each event comes from another—
Success and failure blend with each other.
The future's not here, the past is over,
The present moment is the answer.
Divine is the giver of keys to forever.
As it's delivered, smile, there is meaning!
All is a blessing as we seek the treasure—
Breathe in, breathe out, life's greatest pleasure
Is what we learn on the road to forever!

The Elder Seal

We will not go silently into the night
Losing our minds, our memories, our rights.
Senses diminished, feeling great fright
We must claim our voices, authentic insights.
We are the elders, wisdom keepers of light
We can articulate, speak of this plight.
Silent no more, with our words we alight
Our strength is our wisdom, our numbers, now
fight!
Wisdom keepers, we'll share with delight
Now young ones will listen as we speak of
what's right.
Have faith in the kindness of one another
Trust each person as sister, brother, father and
mother.
Walk in another's shoes, just to feel another
one's suffering is powerful, real!
Reveal the presence of a Higher Power and feel,
The planet earth now must heal.
Living in a place elevated and real
With love, compassion, forgiveness—
This is the elder seal!

Acknowledgements

At times, our own light goes out and is rekindled by a spark from another person. Each of us has cause to think with deep gratitude of those who have lighted the flame within us. Albert Schweitzer

It is with sincere gratitude that we thank the following people for their wisdom, love, support, and encouragement throughout the process of researching, writing, editing, and publishing of this book:

- ♥ The elders of the world, for they are the motivation, inspiration and power behind the program and movement that we call "Onto the Next." We are all part of this exciting journey and evolution called *aging well.*

- ♥ Florence (Linda's Mom) at 91 with dementia, coined the phrase "Onto the Next" shortly after her husband passed on. Her need to let go of possessions and set out on a new journey with music, joy and love, inspired this initiative.

- ♥ Hank (Gretchen's dad), A loving father with great wisdom who continues to inspire!

- ♥ Our parents, those living and deceased.

- ♥ Will Stoler, Linda's husband and partner in Brainysounds, LLC, Onto the Next, and life. Without his tireless efforts, passionate inspiration and editorial input this book would never have seen the light of day!

- ♥ Jack, Gretchen's supportive partner in life's valleys and mountaintop experiences as well as her creative endeavors.

♥ Peter Bruce Wilder-Director of marketing, graphic design and creative consultant. Peter is a virtuoso musician, and Emmy Award-winning composer, photographer, technical engineer and recording master. His unwavering commitment and creative input has been a vital component of this initiative for over fifteen years.

♥ Nancy Quatrano-Editor and publisher who molded, shaped and motivated the final heavy-lifting that this powerful book required. She has become a core member of our family and team.

♥ Our immediate friends and family—you know who you are.

♥ Our new like-minded friends who we connected with in our "Transforming Your Aging Brain" (TYAB) seminars.

♥ Our ever-expanding TYAB community that has helped us on our personal journey of discovery and continues to inspire us to evolve.

About The Authors: Our Stories

Photo by Glenn Moody
http://www.glennmoodyphotography.com/

Linda S. Stoler, M.A., CCC-SLP

As a child, I was painfully shy. In school, although I knew the correct answers, I hoped the teacher would not call on me as I tried to melt into the wooden chair attached to my desk. I was terrified to speak in front of the class. In college and graduate school, I wouldn't sleep the night before I had to make a speech in public speaking classes. I became a speech-language pathologist so that I could find my own voice and help children and adults find theirs.

As a speech-language pathologist, I developed programs for children based on what I had learned in graduate school. Using a left brain, logical, cognitive perspective, I played games, had children repeat sounds and hoped for successful outcomes. However, none of these methods seemed relevant to what the children were learning in their classrooms, and the carryover of new sounds and concepts was negligible.

After fifteen frustrating years that included going through a divorce, I decided to take a much needed break from my career. I hiked the mountains of Vermont, lived in a cabin by a river, wrote poetry and songs, did theater and art and took a sign language class. I began to get in touch with my authentic, creative, spiritual self. When I returned to work as a speech language pathologist, I created original songs and choreographed dances, combining them with American Sign Language and some simple yoga practices to help children more thoroughly acquire early language and literacy skills.

Along with another speech pathologist, we brought special needs and typically developing children out from behind their desks, sparking their individual creative spirits, to participate in multi-modal language learning circles. There was an immediate groundswell of excitement throughout the classrooms and the schools I worked in. Children learned "The Opposite Hop," "The Adverbial Waltz," "The Synonym Twist," and other songs and dances to facilitate sound and language acquisition. Not only was this "whole body learning" received with joy and excitement, but the children acquired better attention, memory and processing skills. Communication improved rapidly. In addition, the children exhibited greater self-esteem and motivation, with fewer behavior problems. This was a winning formula that was noticed and appreciated by parents, educators, administrators and children.

Acquiring learning through music, movement, and manual motion or sign language also resulted in enhanced creativity. By combining cognitive, social-emotional, physical and spiritual components into an all-encompassing practice, we developed a method to create a harmonious balance for the children. Whole classrooms and schools participated in this new approach. I began offering trainings and seminars for children and educators, creating hundreds of circles throughout the United States. I was no longer afraid to speak in front of groups. I had written many lyrics and collaborated with an Emmy award winning composer, Peter Bruce Wilder, producing four CDs. I also produced several teaching manuals.

Three years ago, after my father passed on, my 91-year-old mother with progressive dementia came to live with me. She had been an educator, poet and songwriter herself. I began taking her to some of my circles with children and teachers. I immediately noticed that her communication skills improved dramatically. She was remembering many songs and learning some signs. She was visibly happier and continued to communicate better. It was at this point that I had an epiphany! My development of music, movement, and manual motion were perfect tools for an aging population!

I began offering multi-generational classes in the Multi-Modal Method in St. Augustine Beach, Florida. Babies, mothers, and grandmas gathered twice each month to sing, dance, and learn sign language. It was an exciting and valuable experience for all. We were creating community and proving that the Multi-Modal Method using music, dance, sign language and meditation are powerful tools to enhance and transform the aging brain! When my mother required memory care, I visited her regularly and began to utilize my methodology with groups of other residents in her facility. The music, movement, sign language, meditation and visualization techniques had remarkable results. People who had been virtually silent, began to sing, move and respond with sincere smiles and joy! I was captivated and motivated to pursue my work with aging seniors.

I have always been interested in the biological and clinical aspects of brain function as they relate to this methodology. My experience affirmed that children and aging adults' brains were evolving in positive and powerful ways through the use of these alternative practices.

The latest neuroscience is showing us how the brain, due to neuroplasticity, changes throughout life. This past year, I conducted seminars, "Transforming Your Aging Brain" to enhance holistic wellness and minimize the risk of dementia and Alzheimer's. I added yoga and other compatible techniques to include exercise, diet and healthy lifestyle changes in order to strengthen and expand a foundation for holistic and healthy aging. A variety of participants attended these classes: those with memory problems, depression, eating disorders, brain tumors, strokes and others in need of an educational, psychological, spiritual and emotional tune-up to awaken and sustain holistic brain wellness. The results were exciting and enlightening. People were using the MMM practice to transform their aging brains! They were moving "Onto the Next!"

Photo by Will Stoler, 2014

Gretchen L. Espinetti, Ph.D

Born on the seacoast of Maine to parents of Swedish and French roots, my family moved to the seacoast of New Hampshire when I was six. Growing up on the coastline of the Atlantic provided me a deep appreciation for the beauty, force, and depth of the mighty sea, and one of my favorite poems, *I Must Go Down to the Sea Again*, by John Masefield.

I have enjoyed an extensive career in bilingual education and early childhood education, spent in many educational settings from P-16 throughout the United States as well as in three countries in Asia. Like Linda, I share a love for languages and literacy. My doctoral studies were grounded in multicultural education with a focus on the Third Culture Kid-(TCK) phenomenon. Very simply, TCKs are children who have spent a significant part of their developmental years outside the parent's cultures.

Although I have traveled extensively throughout the world, for the past six years my work in Florida has been in the health and fitness industry, mostly with seniors over 60. It is in this arena that I was fortunate enough to meet Linda. From the beginning of our encounters at the

160

health and fitness club, we engaged in an amazing depth of discussion, speaking to each other frequently, comparing notes and care ideas for our aging parents and their stages of dementia. We realized rather quickly our common needs and focus. The void that exists in these areas of care is filled by the information in this book and has put a new fire into my research interests and passion for the field of neuroscience—particularly as this field applies to our aging population.

Over the span of thirty-plus years in the education field, I have pondered many questions about the brain, multilingualism, language and literacy learning in general. In my teaching, I used many non-traditional methods and approaches including music, movement, drama, sign language, and art in the first and multiple language learning processes. In my research I discovered that neuroscience has revealed that being fluent in more than one language protects us against age-related cognitive declines. It affects the structural plasticity of the brain. And, according to Dr. Ellen Bialystok at York University in Toronto, regular use of at least two languages or more appears to delay the onset of Alzheimer's disease symptoms. The whole brain appears to rewire because of multiple languages and makes our brains stronger! This has been a powerful realization and supports my theory of the importance of multiple-language acquisition at early ages!

Five years ago, I decided to leave my education career (of over thirty years) to finish writing my dissertation on the *third culture kid* phenomenon and pursue a more peaceful, simpler life, near the ocean once again. After adventuring across the diverse lands of Florida, I arrived on the Atlantic coast of Florida, which reminded me very much of my homeland along the New Hampshire coastline. During this time of reflection and writing, I managed to reinvent myself within the health and fitness industry.

In my current position as a General Manager at a regional health and fitness facility, our members represent a mostly "over 60" population. I observe the aging process on a daily basis as well as the ongoing physical, emotional, social, cognitive, and spiritual needs of the aging brain.

Two years ago, just having graduated with my PhD, I received one of those devastating phone calls. I was fortunate to be with my mother for the last seven days of her life. She passed away unexpectedly from cancer, leaving my father alone and lost, and questioning his purpose in life now without his beloved wife of many years. Shortly after my mother's death, my dad made a major decision to move to Florida to be near me. I have observed his physical, social, emotional, and cognitive decline over the past two years, with two major hospitalizations and much time in skilled nursing facilities in the last year and, most recently, a diagnosis of early dementia.

What I find most helpful in being his "care partner," is using the Multi-Modal Method (MMM) tools that Linda describes and illustrates so very clearly in our "Transforming Your Aging Brain" seminars—especially music, movement, and a meditation/quiet time with him. When my father is actively engaged in the MMM practice, he is more alert, less confused, and more content in the moment. His intellectual-self returns which brings him (and me) joy and gratitude. I feel like he is fully with me. Also, asking him direct questions about his life gives him an opportunity to tell the many chapters of his life story (one of his strengths) with vivid reminiscing.

Over the last twelve years, I have also experienced the loss of two aunts, a best friend's mother, and another friend's father to Alzheimer's disease. These sad passings of special people have affected me deeply and stimulated me to learn how to promote positive brain health and wellness for myself and others. Recently, the only uncle left in our family, my father's brother, has been diagnosed with dementia.

All of these special loved ones have reignited my interest in the brain and especially the plasticity of this powerful organ. I am convinced we CAN transform our aging brains through the MMM practice.

References

Amen, D.G. (2013). *Unleash the Power of the Female Brain*. New York: Harmony Books.

Amen, D.G. (1999). *Change Your Brain, Change Your Life*. New York: Three Rivers Press.

AARP Bulletin, June/July 2013, Washington, DC.

Begley, S. (2007). *Train Your Mind, Change Your Brain*. New York: Ballantine Books.

Benson, H. (2013). Retrieved from: www.massgeneral.org

Bergland, Christopher (2013) http://www.psychologytoday.com/blog/the-athletes-way/201310/why-is-dancing-so-good-your-brain

Bialystok, E. Speaking multiple languages may help delay dementia symptoms, April 2012 on www.npr.org

Bolte-Taylor, J. (2009). *My Stroke of Insight*. New York: Penguin Books.

Campbell, D. (2001). *Mozart Effect*. New York: Harper Collins.

Carson, S. (2012). *Your Creative Brain*. San Francisco: Jossey Bass.

Chopra, D. & Tanzi, R.E. (2012). *Super Brain: Unleashing the explosive power of your mind to maximize health, happiness and spiritual well-being*. New York: Harmony Books.

Cohen, G. (2000). *The Creative Age: Awakening human potential in the second half of life*. New York: Harper Collins.

Cohen, G. (2005). *The Mature Mind: The positive power of the aging brain*. New York: Basic Books.

Collier, S. (2013). Retrieved from: www.creativepathtogrowth.com

Damasio, A. (2003). *Looking for Spinoza*. Orlando: Harcourt Books.

Davidson, R.J. (2008). Buddha's Brain: Neuroplasticity and meditation, *IEEE Signal Magazine*, 25 (1), 174-176.

Dispenza, J. (2012). *Breaking the Habit of Being Yourself.* Hay House Publishers.

Dychtwald, K. & Kadlec, D. (2009). *With Purpose: Going from success to significance in work and life.* William Morrow Publishers.

Erickson, K. *Better Nutrition*, November 2013.

Fehmi, L. (2007). *The Open-Focus Brain.* Boston: Trumpeter.

Ferguson, R.C., Zubko, A. (1996). Treasury of Spiritual Wisdom.India: Shri Jainendra Press

Fishman, T. (2010). *Shock of Gray.* New York: Scribner.

Fleming, S.M. (2010). University College, London.

Fotuhi, M. (2003). *The Memory Cure.* New York: McGraw-Hill.

Fox, M. (2004). *Creativity.* New York: Penguin Books.

Furst, B. (2013). Conscious Remembering. Retrieved from: www.youcanremember.com

George, B. (2007). *True North.* San Francisco: Jossey Bass.

Goleman, D. (1994). *Emotional Intelligence.* New York: Bantam Books.

Goleman, D. (2013). *Focus: The hidden driver of excellence.* New York: Harper Collins.

Hahn, Thich Nhat and Wietske Vriezen (2008) *Mindful Movements: Ten Exercises for Well-Being*

Hancock, J. & Buggy, C. (2012). *Successful Memory Techniques.* New York: McGraw Hill.

Hanson, R. Being for Yourself. Retrieved from: www.podgallery.org

Hanson, R. (2011). Your Wise Brain. Retrieved from: www.psychologytoday.com

Hunt, V. (1996). *Infinite Mind.* Malibu Publishing.

Kramer, A. et al. (2006). Exercise, cognition, and the aging brain. *Journal of Applied Physiology*, 101 (4), 1237-1242.

Lesser, L.K. (2013). Retrieved from: www.returntooursenses.com

Marshall, L. (2013). The Better Brain Diet: Eat right to stay sharp. Retrieved from: www.naturalawakenings.com

Mercola, J.M. (2013). Retrieved from: www.mercola.com

Merzenich, M. (2013). *Soft Wired: How the new science of brain plasticity can change your life.* San Francisco: Parnassus.

Newberg, A. & Waldman, M. (2009). *How God Changes Your Brain*. New York: Ballantine Books.

Nishiyama, Y. (2013). Counting with the Fingers. *International Journal of Pure and Applied Mathematics*, 85 (5), 859-868.

Northrop, Christine, MD (PBS Special) www.pbs.org.

Paturel, A., (2013) Yoga in Your Seventies, *AARP Magazine,* October/November, Washington, DC.

Penfield, W. (1952). Memory Mechanisms. *AMA Archives of Neurology and Psychiatry* 67, 178-198.

Perlmutter, D. (2013). Retrieved from: www.perlmutter.com

Pink, D. (2005). *A Whole New Mind.* New York: Penguin Group.

Ram Dass (2013) *Polishing the Mirror.*

Ratey, J. (2001). *A Users Guide to the Brain.* New York: Pantheon Books.

Ratey, J. (2009). *Spark: The revolutionary new science of exercise and the brain.* Little, Brown and Company, New York.

Restak, R. (2013). Retrieved from www.richardrestak.com

Roizen, M. & Oz, M. (2008). *You Being Beautiful.* New York: Free Press.

Rosen, M. Get moving for a healthy brain. *AARP Bulletin*, September 2013.

Seagull, B. (2005). *Mind Your Mind*. Wisconsin: Attainment Company.

Seligman, M.E. (2011). *Flourish: A visionary new understanding of happiness and well-being*. New York: Free Press.

Selver, C. (2007). *Reclaiming Vitality and Presence: Sensory awareness as a practice for life*. Berkeley: North Atlantic Books.

Siegel, D. (2010). *Mindsight*. New York: Bantam Books.

Siegel, D. (2007). *The Mindful Brain*. New York: Norton Books.

Statistics retrieved from: www.alz.org

Tolle, E. (2005). *A New Earth: Awakening to your life's purpose*. New York: Penguin Books.

Tramo, M. J. (2013). Retrieved from: www.brainmusic.org

Turner, L. *Better Nutrition*.

Vaillant, G. (2008). *Spiritual Evolution: How we are wired for faith, hope, and love*. New York: Broadway.

Wenk, G. Retrieved from: www.medicine.osu.edu

White, J. Personal conversation, June 2013.

Williams, M. (1922). "The Velveteen Rabbit". Grosser & Dunlap.

Williamson, M. (2008). *The Age of Miracles*. Hay House Publishers.

Wolpert, D. (2013). Smart moves, motor control, and the brain. Retrieved from: www.kavlifoundation.org

Zinczenko, D. (2012). *Eat This Not That*. New York: Rodale.

Zukov, G. (1989). *The Seat of the Soul*. New York: Simon & Schuster.

Helpful Resources

We have found the following helpful resources relating to the brain, neuroscience, and sign language.

Alzheimer's and Dementia Weekly
Alzheimer's Association website- www.alz.org
Alzheimer's Reading Room
ASLPRO.com
Brain Science Podcasts
Dana Foundation
HandSpeak.com
Lifeprint.com (video sign training)
National Institute of Health (NIH)
Signingsavvy.com
Ted.com (featuring Dr. Stuart Brown, Sir Ken Robinson, *on play, creativity, education and the arts*)
YouTube (featuring Dr. Merzenich, Jon Kabat-Zinn, Dr. Siegel *on neuroplasticity, meditation, mindsight, etc.*)

TRANSFORMING YOUR AGING BRAIN is also available through Amazon.com and can be purchased as an eBook for the Kindle and other readers. For more information, visit www.transformyouragingbrain.com.

For more information about the TYAB seminars, visit: www.ontothenext.org